THE DOCTRINE OF CHRIST

By

Derek R Aylward

For the broken in spirit
who are still searching for the goodness...

May you discover
that love was closer than you ever imagined.

Why This Book Exists...

The Doctrine of Christ
was never meant to stay a doctrine.

It was meant to become a life.

Not something you visit on Sundays.
Not something you agree with in theory.

But something you walk in until it begins to carry
you.

Many know the words.

Few know the way.

Because the way cannot just be memorized.

It must be entered.

And once entered...
it changes everything.

This is that doorway.

The Doctrine Of Christ
By Derek R. Aylward

Published by Body of Christ Creative
bodyofchrist.online

Scripture quotations are drawn from various Bible translations and are used for inspirational and educational purposes.

Printed and distributed by IngramSpark.

First published in Australia, 2026

For more resources, teachings, and related works, visit bodyofchrist.online

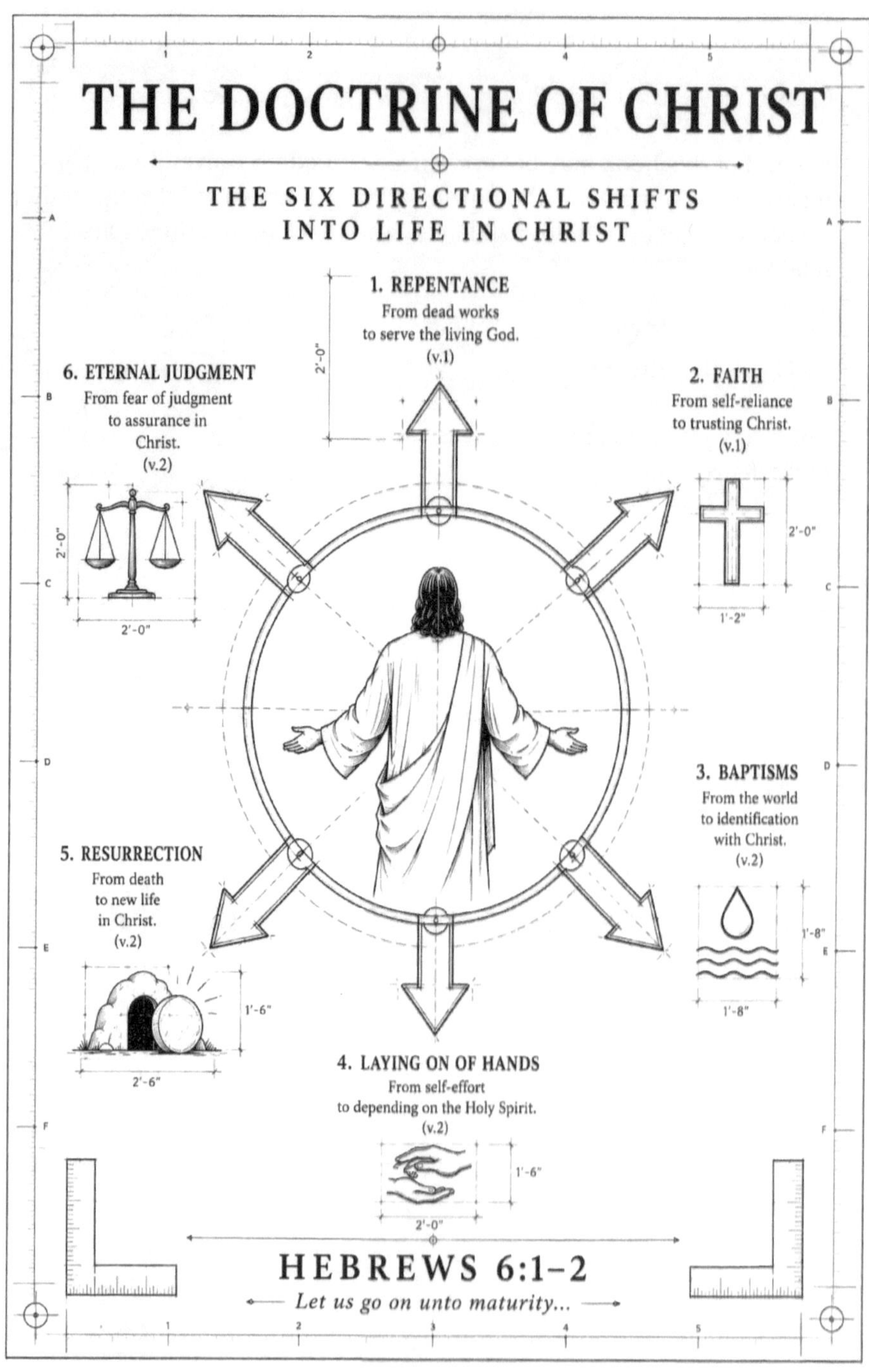

THE DOCTRINE OF CHRIST
THE SIX DIRECTIONAL SHIFTS
INTO LIFE IN CHRIST
1. REPENTANCE
From dead works
to serve the living God.
(v.1)
6. ETERNAL JUDGMENT
From fear of judgment
to assurance in
Christ.
(v.2)
2. FAITH
From self-reliance
to trusting Christ.
(v.1)
3. BAPTISMS
From the world
to identification
with Christ.
(v.2)
5. RESURRECTION
From death
to new life
in Christ.
(v.2)
4. LAYING ON OF HANDS
From self-effort
to depending on the Holy Spirit.
(v.2)
HEBREWS 6:1-2
Let us go on unto maturity...

BOOK 2
THE DOCTRINE OF CHRIST

INTRODUCTION

The Doctrine of Christ. The Six Directional Shifts Into Life In Christ

Core Scripture
Hebrews 6:1–2

Therefore leaving the principles of the doctrine of Christ, let us go on unto perfection; not laying again the foundation of repentance from dead works, and of faith toward God,

Of the doctrine of baptisms, and of laying on of hands, and of resurrection of the dead, and of eternal judgment.

There are some truths in Scripture that sit quietly in plain sight.

Not because God hid them,
but because familiarity can make us walk past what we have seen for years.

For many believers, **The Doctrine of Christ** is one of those truths.

It appears in **Hebrews 6:1–2** not as a side note, not as an advanced topic for scholars, and not as an optional extra for the especially serious. It is presented as **foundation**—the kind of foundation a life is meant to be built on.

And yet, for many of us, it has rarely been taught clearly.

For decades, many Christians have been taught *about* Jesus, but not always taught how to recognize the **pattern of life In Christ** that the Scriptures call us to grow into.

We have often been taught salvation as an event,
while maturity was left vague.

We have been told to believe,
but not always shown how belief becomes **direction**.

That is where this book begins.

The Doctrine of Christ is not just what we believe about Jesus.
It is the pattern of life we grow into In Him.

This book is not about religious performance.
It is not about becoming more burdened, more complicated, or more self-conscious.

It is about **direction**.

It is about six foundational shifts that move a person from the planning loops of condemnation, striving, confusion, and self-driven living...
into the living pattern of **God's love In Christ**.

As Paul writes:

"As ye have therefore received Christ Jesus the Lord, so walk ye in him:
Rooted and built up in him, and stablished in the

faith..."
— Colossians 2:6–7 (KJV)

That is the heart of this book.

To become **rooted**.
To become **built up**.
To become established in a life that no longer swings with
every inner storm, but begins to grow from a deeper
support.

Like the roots of a tree.
Like the footings of a house.
Like the hidden structure beneath a life that can finally carry
weight.

If the foundation is unclear, the life built upon it will always
wobble.

But if the foundation is true,
everything changes.

A Forgotten Foundation

In **Hebrews 5**, the writer gives a loving but direct warning:
there comes a time when God's people should no longer
remain spiritual infants. There comes a time when growth
should have produced discernment. There comes a time
when milk is no longer enough.

Then, in **Hebrews 6:1–2**, instead of adding pressure, the
writer points back to the foundation.

Not to shame the reader.
Not to condemn the reader.
But to make something plain:

If we are going on unto maturity, we must understand what maturity is built on.

Then he names the six foundations:

- Repentance from dead works

- Faith toward God

- The doctrine of baptisms

- Laying on of hands

- Resurrection of the dead

- Eternal judgment

These are not random topics.

They are not disconnected theological boxes to tick.

They form a **living progression**—a movement from old patterns into a new way of being. A journey from inherited confusion into spiritual clarity. A pathway out of self-driven life and into the structure of Christ.

That is how this book approaches them.

Not merely as doctrines to study,
but as **six directional shifts** into life **In Christ**.

The writer also says... ***"Not laying again"***

These 6 teachings were what catapulted the early church from a backwater movement to the influence we still see today.

They are the glue that held the early church together when there were no Gospels or New Testament to guide them.

Why This Doctrine Matters...

Many people are not just battling sin.
They are battling **cycles**.

Cycles of regret.
Cycles of striving.
Cycles of overthinking.
Cycles of trying harder, failing again, then starting over
beneath the weight of condemnation.

Some have lived in these loops for so long that they mistake
them for normal Christian life.

But much of what we call "struggle" is not actually growth.

It is often the soul circling the same ground,
trying to produce life from a direction that cannot give it.

That is why The Doctrine of Christ matters.

Because these six foundations are not just truths to
memorize.
They are **turnings**.

They show us how to stop circling.
They show us how to face a new direction.
They show us how body, soul, and spirit begin to come into
alignment under the life of Christ.

This is not maturity by pressure.

This is maturity by **pattern**.

And the pattern is always found **In Christ**.

The Six Directional Shifts Into Life In Christ

This book expands on the six foundation stones of
Hebrews 6 as six directional shifts that move a person
from the planning loops of condemnation into the living
architecture of God's love.

Chapter 1 — Repentance

Turning from the planning loops of condemnation into a
new direction of life

Repentance is not merely feeling bad about what has
happened.
It is a heartfelt change in direction.
It is the moment a person stops circling dead ground and
begins to turn toward what is true.

Chapter 2 — Faith Toward God

Anchoring the body, soul, and spirit toward God's love as
the true source of support

Faith is more than agreement with an idea.
It is the reorientation of trust.
It is where the whole person begins to lean away from self-
sourcing and toward the Father as the true support of life.

Chapter 3 — The Doctrine of Baptisms

The full immersion of body, soul, and spirit into the life and
pattern of Christ

Baptism is more than a ceremony remembered.
It is a revelation of immersion.
This chapter explores the deeper pattern of being fully
immersed into Christ—body, soul, and spirit—so life is no
longer lived from the old centre.

Chapter 4 — Laying On of Hands

The shift from self-driven living into the power, support, and transmission of community

God never designed us to mature alone.
This foundation reveals more than ritual.
It reveals blessing, support, impartation, and the shared life of the Body of Christ.

Chapter 5 — Resurrection of the Dead

The emergence of new daily patterns as the life of Christ rises within us

Resurrection is not only future hope.
It is also present pattern.
Old ways die. New ways rise.
This chapter explores how the life of Christ begins to appear in daily rhythms, desires, habits, and responses.

Chapter 6 — Eternal Judgment

Understanding the blueprints of heaven, accountability, and the lasting architecture of what is true

Judgment is often feared because it is misunderstood.
But eternal judgment is not merely about punishment.
It is about ultimate truth, divine order, accountability, and what remains when everything false is stripped away.

Not Just Doctrine... Direction

This book is called *The Doctrine of Christ,* but its purpose is not to hand you six cold doctrines to admire from a distance.

Its purpose is to help you see the **pattern In Christ** more clearly.

Because doctrine, in its truest sense, is not meant to sit on a shelf.

It is meant to shape a life.

It is meant to reveal what direction you are facing.

Because what we keep facing,
we eventually follow.

And what we keep following,
we eventually become.

That is why these six foundations matter so deeply.

They are not merely things to know.
They are movements that reorient the whole person.

Out of death and into life.
Out of confusion and into clarity.
Out of self-driven effort and into the living support of God's love.

A Warm Invitation Before We Begin

If you have spent years in church and still feel like
something foundational was never fully explained...
you are not alone.

If you have loved God and yet still found yourself caught in
patterns you could not name...
you are not alone.

If you have sensed there must be a deeper structure beneath
the Christian life than "try harder and do better"...
you are not alone.

This book is not written to overwhelm you.

It is written to help you **see**.

To slow down.
To notice what direction your life is facing.
To recognize the patterns that have shaped you.
And to discover the quiet, powerful architecture of life **In Christ**.

So as you begin, do not rush.

This is not a race to finish a book.
It is an invitation to let the foundation speak.

Read slowly.
Reflect honestly.
Let the questions do their work.

And as each chapter unfolds, may you not only understand **The Doctrine of Christ** more clearly...

May you begin to feel the direction of life itself shifting beneath your feet.

Welcome to the journey.

CHAPTER 1 — REPENTANCE FROM DEAD WORKS

Turning from what cannot give life... to the living flow of God's love In Christ.

Chapter Core Scripture — Hebrews 6:1 (KJV)

"Therefore leaving the principles of the doctrine of Christ, let us go on unto perfection; not laying again the foundation of repentance from dead works, and of faith toward God."

Chapter Introduction

Repentance is often misunderstood.

Many hear the word and think of guilt, regret, or being told to look backward. But in the doctrine of Christ, repentance is not about being trapped in the past—it is about recognizing that the path you are on is not leading to life, and choosing a better direction. It is not punishment; it is mercy. It is not the weight of failure; it is the doorway into change.

A person can be busy, sincere, and even well-intentioned... and still be building a life that does not produce peace.

The Bible calls this **dead works**—not merely wrong actions, but ways of living that are disconnected from the source of life itself.

When life is drawn from the wrong source, the soul begins to strive, repeat, and carry pressure it was never designed to hold.

To help us see this clearly, we will walk through one of the most powerful pictures Jesus gave—the story of **the Father and the two sons**. In this story, we do not just see one kind of lostness, but two: one son who runs away, and another who stays but lives without rest.

Both reveal something deeply human. And through them, we begin to see that repentance is not about going backward —it is about turning toward life.

Section Overview

1. A Hell of Our Own Making
We begin by exposing how dead works create an inward life of striving, pressure, and exhaustion. Before many people fear hell later, they are already living in a kind of inner torment now—trying to draw life from what cannot give it.

2. The Call to Turn
Through the story of the younger son, we see what repentance looks like in motion—distance, emptiness, and the moment he "comes to himself" and begins the journey home.

3. Where This Path Is Showing Up in You
The story becomes personal. We recognize the same patterns of striving, fear, and self-protection in our own lives—whether we have run far or remained outwardly faithful.

4. From Striving to Life

We return to the story through the Father's response. Here we see the difference between servanthood and sonship, and how life is restored not through effort, but through relationship.

5. What Direction Are You Really Facing?

The chapter closes with a moment of honest reflection. Not perfection, but direction—because repentance is ultimately revealed in the way the heart is turning.

To live In Christ is to flow in the anointed presence of God's love like Jesus.

So before asking how far you've gone...
the better question is this:

Which way are you facing?

Section 1 — A Hell of Our Own Making

Repentance is the moment truth becomes stronger than appetite...

Core Scripture — Hebrews 6:1 (KJV)

"Therefore leaving the principles of the doctrine of Christ, let us go on unto perfection; not laying again the foundation of...

Repentance... from dead works, and of faith toward God."

Many people hear the word **repentance** and immediately think of regret.

They think of guilt.
They think of shame.
They think of being told to look backward.
They think of being scolded for what went wrong.

But that is often where the confusion begins.

Biblically, repentance is not about becoming trapped in the past. It is about recognizing that the path you are on is not leading to life... and choosing a better direction.

That matters deeply, because if repentance is taught as punishment, the soul will resist it.
But if repentance is understood as mercy, the heart can respond.

This is why the first words in this foundation matter so much: repentance from dead works.

The emphasis is not on becoming obsessed with what is dead.
The emphasis is on recognizing what is not giving life... so you can stop feeding it.

And for many people, that recognition is more urgent than they realize.

Because before many people ever ask, *"Am I going to hell?"* they are already living in one.

Not necessarily a place of fire in the future...
but an inward life of pressure, striving, fear, repetition, and soul exhaustion in the present.

That is where this chapter begins.

Not with accusation...
but with recognition.

Repentance from dead works is the turning point where we stop trying to draw life from what cannot give it. And in the light of Christ, we can say it even more clearly:

A dead work is any work that is disconnected from the living flow of God's love.

Before a person can truly turn, they must first see the path they are on.

1. When the Wrong Path Feels Normal

One of the hardest things to recognize in life is a pattern that looks productive.

A person can be moving constantly and still be going nowhere.

They can be making plans, solving problems, setting goals, managing pressure, and pushing forward... yet inwardly remain trapped in the same emotional and spiritual condition.

That is what makes dead works so deceptive.

They do not always look rebellious.
They often look responsible.

They can look like:

- trying harder

- fixing the same issue again

- proving yourself one more time

- holding everything together

- overthinking what went wrong

- promising yourself that next time will be different

For a moment, that movement can feel like progress.

But if the **source** has not changed, the cycle simply begins again.

This is why many people feel like they are always "working on themselves," yet never arriving in peace.

They are moving.
But they are not being led into life.

A path can feel familiar, productive, and even sincere...
while still leading nowhere life can grow.

2. What Dead Works Actually Are

A dead work is not simply a bad action.

That is where many people misunderstand the phrase.

A dead work can be sinful.
It can be self-protective.
It can be prideful.
It can be fear-driven.

But it can also look noble, spiritual, disciplined, or responsible on the outside.

The issue is not merely what the hands are doing.
The issue is what the life is connected to.

A work becomes dead when it is disconnected from the living source of God. And because this book is leading us toward the real destination, we can say it plainly:

A dead work is any work that is disconnected from the living flow of God's love.

That means two people can do the same outward thing...
but not from the same spirit.

One gives from love.
Another gives to be accepted.

One serves from overflow.
Another serves to prove their worth.

One obeys from trust.
Another obeys from fear.

One waits in peace.
Another performs under pressure.

The outward motion may look similar.
But heaven reads deeper than appearances.

This is why Jesus said life is not produced by the flesh alone, and why the doctrine begins here.

Because a person can spend years doing "good things" outwardly... while inwardly living under the crushing burden of self-salvation.

Dead works are not just wrong behaviors.

They are **repeated patterns** of trying to produce life without remaining connected to the living flow of God's love.

3. Why the Soul Keeps Repeating the Cycle

The soul is not the enemy.

The soul has a job.

Its role is to interpret, respond, remember, and protect.
It learns from pain.
It watches for patterns.
It tries to keep us safe.

That is not wrong.
That is part of how we were made.

But when the soul is not clearly anchored in what is truly life-giving, it starts protecting the wrong things.

It may protect:

- image instead of truth

- comfort instead of growth

- control instead of trust

- approval instead of peace

- performance instead of love

Over time, these patterns become so familiar that they begin to feel like identity.

A person may say... *"This is just how I am."*

But often, what they are calling personality...
is actually adaptation.

The soul does not like uncertainty.
It does not like helplessness.
It does not like not knowing how things will turn out.

So it creates movement.

- If I can just do more...

- If I can just think harder...

- If I can just fix the outcome...

- If I can just be enough...

- If I can just get it right next time...

But this is where striving becomes a trap.

Because the soul can generate motion.
It can generate effort.
It can generate temporary relief.

But it cannot generate true life on its own.

That is why repentance is not merely behavioral.
It is directional. It is the moment a person begins to realize:
"The thing I keep using to save myself... is the very thing
keeping me tired."

The soul can be a powerful servant, but it was never meant
to decide what gives life.

4. How Striving Becomes an Inner Hell

Striving is exhausting because it never fully settles the heart.

Even when it seems to "work" for a moment, the peace does not last.

You achieve the goal... but the ache remains.
You fix the issue... but the fear returns.
You get through the day... but the pressure starts again tomorrow.

Why?

Because dead works can manage symptoms...
but they cannot heal roots.

They can create the appearance of control.
They can produce short bursts of relief.
They can keep a person busy enough to avoid deeper questions.

But they cannot remove the inner burden of trying to become whole by your own strength.

This is where many people begin living in what feels like an inner courtroom.

They replay conversations.
They relive failures.
They rehearse what they should have done.
They make fresh promises to themselves.
They vow to do better next time.

And the result is not freedom.

It is self-judgment.

This is the cycle of condemnation.

Condemnation is not merely feeling bad about something.
It is the inward pressure of trying to justify yourself without resting in life.

And this is why the title of this section matters:

A Hell of Our Own Making.

Not because God delights in torment.
Not because He is eager to cast people away.
But because when life is drawn from the wrong source, the soul can build its own prison.

It can become a life of:

- endless pressure

- endless self-correction

- endless inner accusation

- endless rehearsing

- endless trying

- endless fatigue

And all the while, the person may still call it "being responsible," "being committed," or even "being faithful."

But if the fruit is pressure without peace...
effort without rest...
movement without life... something deeper is wrong.

When life is drawn from the wrong source, the soul can build a prison and call it maturity.

5. The First Mercy Is Seeing It

The good news is this:

Repentance does not begin with punishment.
It begins with light.

The first mercy of God is often not instant escape from the cycle. It is the ability to finally see it.

You begin to notice what is driving you.
You begin to recognize the patterns.
You begin to see how much of your movement has been fueled by fear, pain, pressure, or the need to feel secure.

This can feel confronting at first.
But it is actually kindness. Because what can be seen can be brought into truth. And what is brought into truth can be turned.

This is why repentance must be taught gently.

It is not God saying,
"Look how badly you have failed."

It is God saying,
"You do not have to keep living like this."

That is a very different voice.

And that is why repentance from dead works is not the beginning of condemnation.

It is the beginning of mercy.

It is the moment the heart begins to recognize:

- this path is not giving life

- this pressure is not peace

- this effort is not rest

- this cycle is not freedom

- this source is not love

And from that recognition, a new direction becomes possible.

Repentance begins when the heart finally sees that what it has been feeding cannot give it life.

Guided Discovery

Take a moment before moving forward—the key is found in the reflection.

This is not a place to judge yourself.
It is simply a place to see.

Let the questions guide you gently.

1. Where in your life do you keep increasing effort… yet still not arrive in peace?
Sometimes more effort feels like progress, but if peace never settles, the source may not be life-giving.

2. In what situations have you mistaken pressure for responsibility?
What feels like maturity on the surface can sometimes be fear trying to stay in control underneath.

3. What patterns in your thinking, relationships, or habits look productive... but leave you inwardly tired?
Not everything that moves forward is actually leading into life.

4. Where have you been managing symptoms instead of allowing God to reveal the source?
Surface fixes can feel helpful for a moment, but they rarely bring lasting rest.

5. Can you see any place where the soul has built a prison and called it maturity, discipline, or faithfulness?
What feels strong on the outside can sometimes be quietly exhausting on the inside.

6. Is it possible that some of your "trying to do better" has been striving disconnected from God's love?
When the source is wrong, even sincere effort can leave the heart weary.

And if that is true... can you feel the mercy in realizing that repentance is not punishment, but an invitation to turn? This is not about being pushed backward—it is about being called into life.

Bridge

These are not questions of rejection.
They are questions of recognition.

Because the moment you can truly see the path…
you are no longer completely trapped inside it.

What is seen in truth can begin to turn toward life.

Repentance from dead works is not a call to obsess over the past.
It is not another burden to carry.
And it is not a demand to punish yourself into change.

It is the mercy of God revealing that you do not have to keep trying to draw life from what cannot give it.

A dead work is any work that is disconnected from the living flow of God's love.

And to live **In Christ** is not to take on a heavier religious load.

To live In Christ is to flow in the anointed presence of God's love like Jesus.

That is the direction.
That is the difference.

And once the heart begins to see that the old path is not life…
the next question is no longer:

"What is wrong with me?"

The next question becomes:

Who is calling me to turn… and what does that turn really look like?

SECTION 2 — THE CALL TO TURN

Repentance is the moment home becomes visible again.

Anchor Scripture... **The Prodigal Son.**

"And when he came to himself, he said, How many hired servants of my father's have bread enough and to spare, and I perish with hunger!"
— Luke 15:17 (KJV)

There are moments in life when the soul runs so far on appetite, emotion, pride, or pain that it forgets where home is.

Not always physical home.
Not always even a place.

Sometimes home is the place in you where truth still lives.
The place where the Father's order still makes sense.
The place where peace is not forced, and love is not earned.

That is why Jesus gave us the story of the younger son.

Because repentance is not easiest to understand as a doctrine.
It is easiest to understand as a person who went too far...
and finally realized he did not have to stay there.

This is the call to turn.

Not merely to feel bad.
Not merely to admit failure.
Not merely to cry in the pigpen.

But to see clearly enough to rise...
and move in a new direction.

1. The Younger Son's Path Always Begins by Looking Away

The younger son did not begin in rebellion because he wanted pain.

He began because distance looked like freedom.

He wanted his portion.
He wanted movement.
He wanted independence.
He wanted life on his own terms.

That is what sin often feels like in the beginning.
Not like darkness.
Like possibility.

Not like death.
Like choice.

The path away from the Father rarely introduces itself as destruction.
It introduces itself as self-definition.

It whispers:

You do not need to stay under this order.
You do not need to wait.
You do not need to trust.
Take what is yours and build your own life.

This is the same old pattern.

It is the pattern of Adam.
It is the pattern of self-direction apart from God.
It is the path of taking instead of trusting.
It is the beginning of dead works.

The younger son did not just leave a house.
He left a covering.

He stepped away from source, order, relationship, and
provision.
And for a while, it probably felt exciting.

Many dead works begin that way.

They begin with energy.
They begin with confidence.
They begin with the illusion that appetite knows where life
is.

But appetite is a terrible compass.

It can point to what feels urgent...
while leading you away from what is true.

And that is why repentance must begin with more than
emotion.

It begins when truth becomes stronger than appetite.

2. The Famine Reveals What Appetite Could Never Sustain

The younger son spent what had been placed in his hands.

Then the famine came.

That detail matters.

Jesus did not say he merely ran out.
He said **"there arose a mighty famine in that land"**
(Luke 15:14).

In other words, the external environment changed…
and suddenly what looked strong was exposed as weak.

This is how many people discover dead works.

Not at the beginning.
At the collapse.

When the relationship fails.
When the body breaks down.
When the money runs dry.
When the plan no longer works.
When the approval stops.
When the distraction loses its power.
When the thing that once fed the soul no longer carries it.

A famine is not always punishment. Sometimes it is
revelation.

It reveals what was never built on true support.
It reveals what could not survive pressure.
It reveals what we leaned on instead of the Father.

The younger son had enough while conditions were easy.
But easy conditions can hide weak foundations.

Pressure tells the truth.

And the famine did not create his emptiness.
It uncovered it.

That is important.

Because many people blame the hard season for what the
hard season merely exposed.

The storm did not invent the crack in the wall.
It revealed it.

A carpenter knows the difference...

So does the Spirit.

The famine is often where repentance begins to whisper.
Not because God delights in pain— but because pain has a
way of silencing lies.

3. Emptiness Is Often the First Honest Messenger

The younger son moved from independence to desperation.

He joined himself to a citizen of that country.
He was sent into the fields to feed swine.
And Jesus tells us something deeply revealing:

"And no man gave unto him."
— Luke 15:16 (KJV)

That line is loaded.

He had pursued a life outside the Father's house.
He had spent himself chasing appetite.
He had attached himself to another system for support.

And when he was empty...

No man gave unto him.

This is the emotional and spiritual shape of dead works.

You keep pouring yourself into something that cannot love
you back.

You keep serving something that cannot feed your spirit.
You keep reaching for relief...
but the thing you reach for has no bread in it.

That is why the image of the pigpen is so powerful.

It is not merely about sin.
It is about misdirected hunger.

He is surrounded by food...
but none of it is truly food for him.

That is the human condition apart from God.

People fill their days.
Fill their minds.
Fill their schedules.
Fill their bodies.
Fill their feeds.
Fill their ambitions.

And still remain hungry. Because not everything that fills
you feeds you. Emptiness is painful.
But emptiness is also clarifying.

When appetite has run its course...
when the soul is tired of pretending...
when the body feels the cost...
when the mind can no longer decorate the dysfunction...

Then the **truth** has room to speak.

Emptiness is often the first honest messenger.

Not the final destination.
But the place where the mask starts to fall.

4. "He Came to Himself" — The Turning Point of Repentance

Then comes one of the most powerful lines Jesus ever spoke:

"And when he came to himself..."
— Luke 15:17 (KJV)

That is repentance in seed form.

Not a sermon.
Not a ritual.
Not a performance.

A moment of awakening.

A moment when the fog breaks.
A moment when truth returns to the center.
A moment when the soul stops arguing with reality.

He came to himself.

That means he had been living outside his right mind.
Outside alignment.
Outside true identity.
Outside the wisdom of the Father's house.

He was still himself in existence— but not himself in truth.

This is what sin does.

It does not just make people do wrong things.
It disorients them.

It pulls them out of alignment with what is real.
It trains them to normalize hunger.
It teaches them to call bondage freedom.
It teaches them to call appetite life.

But then something happens. Truth becomes louder. He remembers.

"How many hired servants of my father's have bread enough and to spare, and I perish with hunger!"

Notice what changed.

The father had not changed.
The house had not changed.
The bread had not changed.

What changed...
was what he could finally see.

This is why repentance is not first about proving sorrow. It is about agreeing with truth. Repentance is the moment truth becomes stronger than appetite, and home becomes visible again.

That is the hinge.

Not perfection.
Not arrival.
Visibility.

He can see home again.

And once home becomes visible...
the path can begin.

5. Turning Toward Home Makes Repentance Visible

The younger son did not stay in the pigpen and call that repentance.

He moved.

"I will arise and go to my father..."
— Luke 15:18 (KJV)

That sentence matters.

Repentance is not complete at recognition alone.
It becomes visible in direction.

You can know the truth...
and still sit still.

You can feel conviction...
and still refuse movement.

You can admire the Father's house from a distance...
and still remain in the field of famine.

But the younger son rose.

He turned inward first—
then he turned outward.

That is the order.

He came to himself.
Then he arose.
Then he went.

This is the pattern of repentance from dead works.

1. Truth interrupts the lie.

2. The heart agrees with what is true.

3. Direction begins to change.

That change may begin quietly.

A prayer.
A confession.
A surrender.
A phone call.
A boundary.
A fast.
A return to the Word.
A decision to stop feeding what is killing you.
A decision to stop calling survival "life."

The first steps home are rarely dramatic. But heaven recognizes direction.

And notice this carefully:

The father ran to him while he was yet a great way off.

That means grace was already moving before the son finished his speech.

Repentance does not earn the Father's embrace.
It turns toward the place where the embrace can be received.

That is why the call to turn is not a threat.

It is mercy.

It is the invitation of love to stop dying in a far country when there is still bread in the Father's house.

6. Where This Story Is Still Happening in Us

The younger son is not just a character in a parable.

He is a mirror. This story is still happening in people every day.

Any time we take what has been given and try to build life apart from the Father... the pattern begins again.

Any time we call appetite wisdom...
the path begins again.

Any time we mistake independence for freedom...
the distance begins again.

And any time pressure reveals that what we built cannot hold us... the famine begins to speak.

That is why repentance must be taught as a living pattern, not just a church word.

Because people are still sitting in modern pigpens:

- striving for approval

- chasing relationships that cannot feed them

- medicating emptiness with distraction

- building identities around performance

- serving systems that use them up

- feeding the soul with noise while the spirit starves

And in the middle of it all, the same call still comes:

Come to yourself.
Remember where the bread is.
Rise.
Turn.
Go home.

This is not condemnation.

This is clarity.

And clarity is mercy when it leads you back to life.

7. The Call to Turn Is the Invitation to Come Home

Repentance is often preached like a courtroom. But Jesus told it like a homecoming. That should tell us something.

The Father is not standing at the edge of the property with folded arms and a list of failures.

He is watching the horizon.

He is looking for movement.

He is looking for direction.

He is looking for the moment when truth becomes stronger than appetite… and a son starts walking home.

This is the call to turn.

Not to become religious.
Not to become impressive.
Not to become self-punishing.

To come home.

To return to source.
To return to covering.
To return to truth.
To return to the place where life is supported by the Father again.

Repentance from dead works is not merely turning from bad behavior.

It is turning from every pattern of self-supported life
that keeps you feeding on what cannot satisfy.

And it begins here:

Not when you have cleaned yourself up.
Not when you have fixed the whole mess.
Not when you feel worthy.

But when you can finally see.

Home is visible again.

Guided Discovery

1. When pressure hits your life, do you keep pushing deeper into the famine—or do you begin to ask what the famine is revealing about your true support?
If pressure only makes you strive harder, you may still be trusting the same system that is starving you.

2. Have you mistaken shame for repentance, when true repentance is actually the moment you agree with truth and begin moving toward the Father?
Shame hides in the pigpen. Repentance rises and starts walking.

3. What in your life feels full on the outside but leaves you hungry on the inside?
Not everything that fills you feeds you. Some things occupy your hands while starving your spirit.

4. Can you identify an area where appetite has been louder than truth?
Appetite speaks in urgency. Truth speaks in clarity. One pulls. The other leads.

5. If home became visible again today, what would your first step toward it look like?
Repentance does not need a grand performance. It needs an honest turn.

Repentance is the moment truth becomes stronger than appetite, and home becomes visible again.

Or simply:

The call to turn is not the sound of rejection—it is the invitation to come home

SECTION 3 — WHERE THIS PATH IS SHOWING UP IN YOU

There comes a moment when the story stops being about someone else.

Core Scripture:
"Keep thy heart with all diligence; for out of it are the issues of life." — **Proverbs 4:23**

"Examine yourselves, whether ye be in the faith..."
— 2 Corinthians 13:5

It is one thing to understand repentance as a doctrine.
It is another thing to recognize the pattern in your own life.

Most people can see the younger son in the far country.
They can see Adam reaching for what was forbidden.
They can see Israel going in circles in the wilderness.
But it is often much harder to see where that same path is
still quietly working in us.

That is where repentance begins to deepen.

Not when we can define it.
Not when we can explain it to someone else.
But when the Spirit of Truth gently puts His finger on our
own direction and says,

This is the path you are walking right now.

That can feel confronting at first.
But this is not the confrontation of condemnation.
It is the mercy of God making the road visible.

Because if the road can be seen, the road can be left.

1. Jesus gives us the story so we can see ourselves safely

Jesus returns us to the younger son again here for a reason.

In the last section, we saw the moment of turning.
But now the story helps us see something even more
personal.

Before the younger son ever began the journey home, the wrong path had already become visible within him.

The far country was not only the place he ran to.
It was the condition he had been living in.

The famine was not only around him.
It had begun to show up inside him.

What once felt like freedom had become emptiness.
What once looked exciting had become exhausting.
What once seemed full of promise no longer carried life.

Then came the turning point:
"And when he came to himself..." *(Luke 15:17)*

That is one of the clearest pictures of repentance in all of scripture.

Not because he had fixed his life.
Not because he had earned his way back.
But because truth became visible again.

He could finally see what the path had done to him.

And this is why Jesus tells the story in this way—so we can see our own path from a safe distance.

We watch the younger son and think,
Of course that road leads to hunger.
Of course that road leaves a man empty.
Of course he needs to go home.

Then the Spirit of Truth gently turns the mirror.

Where is that same path showing up in me?

That is not condemnation.
That is God's love making the road visible again.

Because repentance is not merely turning away from what is wrong.
It is turning back toward the Father's house—back toward life, back toward truth, and back toward what it means to live **In Christ**.

2. This path often hides beneath normal life

One of the reasons dead works are so deceptive is because they do not always look dramatic.

Sometimes they look religious.
Sometimes they look responsible.
Sometimes they look productive.
Sometimes they even look noble.

A person can be busy, sincere, and exhausted all at once, while still moving in the wrong direction.

That is why repentance must go deeper than behavior alone.
It must reach the inner pattern.
The leaning of the heart.
The direction of trust.
The quiet motive beneath the visible action.

A man may work hard because he loves what is true.
Or he may work hard because he is trying to outrun the voice that says he is not enough.

Outwardly, both men may look the same.
But inwardly, they are walking two very different roads.

This is why the doctrine of repentance cannot stop at surface correction.

God is not only asking, *What are you doing?*
He is also asking, *What is driving you?*

That question changes everything.

Because many of the heaviest burdens in life are not carried
by the body.
They are carried by the soul.

And the soul can get so used to striving, proving, defending,
and compensating that it starts calling bondage "normal."

But just because something feels familiar
does not mean it is life.

A familiar path can still be the wrong path.

3. Dead works usually leave a trail

If you want to know where this path is showing up in you,
look at the fruit it keeps producing.

Dead works leave clues.

They tend to produce inner pressure without peace.
Movement without rest.
Effort without life.
Religious language without real freedom.
Planning loops without clear direction.
Condemnation without resolution.

You may find yourself replaying old failures again and again.
You may feel the need to fix everything before you can come
near to God.
You may measure your standing by performance, by
discipline, by visible outcomes, or by whether you feel
strong that day.

You may be trying to earn what can only be received.

That is one of the clearest signs that this path is showing up in you.

Dead works always place the center of gravity back on self.

Even when God is mentioned, the soul is still secretly saying,
It all depends on me.
I have to get this right first.
I have to make myself acceptable.
I have to carry the weight of becoming alive.

But that is not the gospel.
And it is not rest.

The call of Christ is not,
"Fix yourself and then come."
The call of Christ is,
"Come, and I will show you life."

Where the soul is still living under pressure to self-generate righteousness, peace, identity, or worth, repentance is needed.

Not as punishment.
As release.

Repentance is where false support begins to let go, and God's love begins to feel like home again.

4. This path often shows up where appetite is stronger than truth

Repentance is the moment truth becomes stronger than appetite.

That appetite may not always be physical.
It may be emotional.
Mental.
Relational.
Financial.
Even spiritual in appearance.

Sometimes appetite says,
"I need comfort now."
Sometimes it says,
"I need control."
"I need recognition."
"I need to be right."
"I need to protect myself."
"I need to get ahead."
"I need something I can hold onto because I do not know
how to rest in God."

When appetite becomes louder than truth, the soul starts
moving by impulse instead of light. That is how people drift.

Not always through open rebellion.
Often through subtle inward agreements.

A person begins to build decisions around fear rather than
faith.
Around image rather than truth.
Around survival rather than love.
Around pressure rather than peace.

And before long, they are carrying a life that no longer feels
like life.

This is why repentance must be personal.
Because no one else can fully see the little bargains we make
inside ourselves.

No one else hears every silent justification.
No one else knows every private turning of the heart.

But God does.

And because He loves us, He does not leave us hidden from ourselves forever.

He brings light.

Not to shame us,
but to wake us up.

Whatever keeps pulling you away from life is showing you where repentance is needed—because life In Christ is never built on inward bargains with fear.

5. The soul often reveals the direction before the life does

Many people wait until life collapses before they admit they are on the wrong road.

But usually the signs begin much earlier.

The soul knows when it has lost peace.
It knows when it is living divided.
It knows when it is running on pressure instead of grace.
It knows when it is building with strain instead of trust.

You can feel it in the atmosphere within.

Irritation becomes easier.
Patience grows thin.
Love feels heavy.
Prayer feels distant.
Truth becomes something you agree with in principle but are not resting in practically.

The body may keep moving.
The smile may stay in place.
The routines may remain intact.
But inwardly something feels off-center.

That matters.

Because the soul often sends warning signals long before the outer structure begins to crack.

This is one reason Proverbs says to keep the heart with all diligence, because out of it are the issues of life.
Life flows outward from inward direction.

If the inward direction is bent, the outward life will eventually feel the strain.

That is not condemnation.
That is design.

God made us in such a way that truth and life belong together.

So when life begins to feel dry, strained, false, driven, or divided, it is worth asking:
What direction am I really facing?
What story am I agreeing with?
What am I trying to carry that was never meant to rest on me?

These questions are not designed to trap you.
They are designed to uncover the road.

And once the road is uncovered, grace can meet you there.

The strain you feel may be the mercy of God showing you that your soul is facing the wrong way, so He can gently turn you back toward life In Christ.

6. Repentance begins when honesty returns

The younger son "came to himself."

That line is simple, but it carries great depth.

Repentance begins when honesty returns.

Not exaggerated shame.
Not dramatic self-hatred.
Just honesty.

Honesty says,
"This path is not feeding me."
"This direction is costing me peace."
"I keep circling the same place."
"I have called this strength, but it is actually strain."
"I have called this wisdom, but it is really fear."
"I have called this independence, but it is separation."
"I have called this righteousness, but it is self-effort."

That kind of honesty is powerful because it breaks
agreement with illusion.

And once illusion begins to lose its hold, truth becomes
visible again.

Many people delay repentance because they think it means
being crushed.
But in reality, repentance is often the first moment a person
starts breathing properly again.

Because truth is breathable.

Truth does not need to be propped up by performance.
Truth does not need endless self-justification.
Truth does not need image management.
Truth stands on its own.

And the soul that returns to truth begins to return to rest.

That is why repentance is not the loss of life.
It is the recovery of it.

Honesty is often the doorway where God's love first feels
real again.

7. Where this path is showing up is also where grace wants to meet you

This is important.

When God shows you where the wrong path is still active in
you, He is not doing it to push you away.

He is doing it because He wants you free.

The revelation of the problem is already part of the mercy.

Grace does not wait at the finish line.
Grace meets you at the turning.

It meets you in the moment you recognize the loop.
The moment you see the striving.
The moment you admit the weariness.
The moment you stop defending what is not producing life.
The moment you say,
"Father, this path is showing up in me."

That prayer is not failure.
That prayer is movement.

Because repentance does not require you to already be
strong.
It requires you to become willing to face what is true.

And wherever that willingness appears, God is near.

The enemy wants exposure to feel like defeat.
But in Christ, exposure becomes the beginning of healing.

What is brought into the light can be redirected.
What is redirected can be restored.
What is restored can become strength.

So do not fear seeing where this path is showing up in you.

That is not the end of the story.
That is the place where the story begins to change.

Where truth exposes the path, God's love opens the way home.

8. The question is not whether the pattern exists, but whether you will turn

Every person has places where the old path still tries to surface.

That should not surprise us.

We are learning to live in a new direction.
We are learning to move from self-support into God's support.
From condemnation into life.
From reaction into truth.
From inward scattering into inward alignment.

The issue is not whether you have ever felt the pull of the old path.

The issue is what you do when you recognize it.

Do you justify it?
Defend it?
Rename it?
Spiritualize it?
Hide it beneath busyness?

Or do you let truth say what it is?

Repentance keeps the heart soft.
It keeps the soul movable.
It keeps the road to life open.

That is why this section matters so much.

Because if you can see where this path is showing up in you,
then you are no longer walking blind.

And if you are no longer walking blind, you can turn.

That is hope.

Real hope.
Not because you are strong enough to perfect yourself,
but because the Father is faithful enough to lead you home.

The path becomes powerless when it is no longer hidden.

Guided Discovery

1. **Where does life feel most strained in me right now?**
    Often the strain points to a place where I am carrying something in self-effort rather than resting in God's love.

2. **What pattern keeps repeating in my thoughts, reactions, or decisions?**
Repeated inner loops often reveal the direction my soul has been facing.

3. **What am I trying to secure by pressure that can only be received through trust?**
This helps expose where dead works are still pretending to be life.

4. **What appetite, fear, or inner story seems to pull me away from peace?**
Whatever repeatedly pulls me from truth is revealing where repentance is needed.

5. **Can I honestly name the place where this path is showing up in me?**
Naming it in truth is often the first real turn toward freedom and back toward life **In Christ**.

Reinforcement Line:
Repentance begins to deepen when the road is no longer just seen in scripture, but recognized within yourself.

SECTION 4 — FROM STRIVING TO LIFE

When repentance stops being a painful loss... and starts becoming a living return.

Core Scripture

**"For this my son was dead, and is alive again; he
was lost, and is found."**
— *Luke 15:24 (KJV)*

There is a moment in repentance where everything changes.

Not because the person has become perfect.
Not because every consequence has disappeared.
Not because they suddenly understand everything.

But because they have turned.

And once a person truly turns, they are no longer walking
deeper into death.
They are now facing life.

That is the great difference.

Repentance is not merely the act of stopping something bad.
It is the beginning of returning to what is alive.

It is the moment a man stops feeding on what cannot
sustain him
and starts moving again toward what was always meant to
be his true support.

That is why repentance from dead works is not mainly about
behavior management.
It is about direction.

Because dead works can keep a person very busy.
But they can never make him alive.

Only life can do that.
And life is found in God's love, fully revealed **In Christ**.

1. Dead Works Can Look Busy While Still Producing Death

One of the most dangerous things about dead works is that they often do not look dead at first.

They look active.
They look serious.
They look responsible.
They look like effort.
They may even look religious.

A man can be exhausted and still be spiritually stuck.
A woman can be trying very hard and still be moving in circles.
A believer can be deeply sincere and still be living under a system that keeps producing pressure instead of peace.

That is why many people confuse movement with life.

But not all movement is life.

A wheel can spin and never leave the ground.
A soul can strain and never arrive.
A person can work harder and harder while remaining disconnected from the very source that gives life.

This is the tragedy of dead works.

They promise progress,
but they produce weariness.

They promise worth,
but they deepen condemnation.

They promise control,
but they quietly drain joy, peace, and rest.

And if left unchallenged, they can make a person believe that struggle itself is spirituality.

But God never called you to be mastered by striving.

He called you to live.

2. The Prodigal Son Did Not Earn His Way Back—He Returned

This is where the story of the prodigal son becomes even more powerful.

When he turned toward home, he was still carrying the smell of the far country.

He had wasted his inheritance.
He had fed among pigs.
He had rehearsed his speech.
He had already judged himself.

And like so many people trapped in dead works, he was still thinking in terms of earning.

He did not return saying,
"Father, I know who I am."

He returned saying,
"Make me as one of thy hired servants."

He was still thinking in wages.
Still thinking in performance.
Still thinking in rank.
Still thinking in what he might be able to do to justify his return.

That is the language of striving.

Even while walking toward mercy,
his soul was still trying to negotiate.

And many believers do the same.

They begin to turn,
but they still secretly believe they must pay their way back
into peace.

They think:

- "If I can pray enough, maybe I'll feel clean again."

- "If I can work harder, maybe God will accept me again."

- "If I can punish myself enough, maybe I'll deserve to come close."

- "If I can become useful, maybe I can belong."

But the father in the story never agreed with the son's
servant identity.

He interrupted it.

Before the speech could fully land, the father ran.
He embraced.
He covered.
He restored.
He celebrated.

Why?

Because the son's return was not a hiring interview.

It was a resurrection.

"For this my son was dead, and is alive again."

That is repentance.

Not a man clawing his way back into worth.
A son turning toward the source of life.

That is the shift from striving to life.

3. God's Love Restores Identity Faster Than Striving Ever Could

Striving always says:
"Prove yourself first."

God's love says:
"Come home first."

Striving says:
"Earn your place."

God's love says:
"You never stopped being called."

Striving says:
"Fix yourself, then return."

The Father says:
"Return, and I will clothe what striving stripped from you."

This is one of the deepest revelations in repentance.

The human soul often assumes that distance from God must be repaired through personal effort.

But the gospel reveals something better.

Distance is overcome by turning.
Life is restored by receiving.

Identity is awakened by relationship.
And the fullness of that relationship is found **In Christ**.

The prodigal son had a speech.
The father had a robe.

The son had shame.
The father had embrace.

The son had a plan for reduced status.
The father had sandals, a ring, and a feast.

This is how dead works are broken.

Not merely by trying less—
but by seeing more clearly.

By seeing that God is not waiting at the end of the road with
crossed arms and a scorecard.

He is watching the horizon.

He is moved by return.

He is not merely interested in your apology.
He is after your restoration.

Because repentance is not complete when a person admits
they were wrong.
It begins to mature when they receive that they are loved.

That is where life starts to flow again.

4. Life In Christ Is Not Earned by Effort—It Is Entered by Direction

This is why the Doctrine of Christ begins with repentance from dead works and then immediately moves to **faith toward God**.

Because once a person turns away from dead works, the next question becomes:

What am I turning toward?

If repentance only removes the old direction, but does not establish a new one, the soul will often drift back into the familiar.

That is why many people repent emotionally,
but not directionally.

They feel sorry.
They feel convicted.
They feel stirred.
But they do not re-anchor their life in a new source.

And without a new source, the old striving returns.

This is why life must be more than the absence of sin.
It must become the presence of a new pattern.

That pattern is **In Christ**.

To live **In Christ** is not merely to believe certain truths about Jesus from a distance.
It is to begin flowing in the anointed presence of God's love like Jesus.

It is a new support system.
A new source of identity.
A new way of seeing.

A new pattern of response.
A new center.

This is life.

Not self-manufactured peace.
Not image management.
Not spiritual panic dressed up as devotion.

But a real return to the Father through the Son,
where the soul no longer has to perform for belonging.

That is why striving exhausts,
but life restores.

Because striving is powered by fear.
Life **In Christ** is sustained by relationship.

5. Repentance Becomes Beautiful When You Realize It Leads Home

Many people fear repentance because they have only heard
it preached as loss.

Lose the sin.
Lose the pride.
Lose the rebellion.
Lose the old life.
Lose the flesh.

And yes, something is lost. But that is not the deepest truth.
The deeper truth is this: Repentance is beautiful because it
leads home.

It leads out of inner exhaustion.
It leads out of condemnation loops.

It leads out of self-punishment.
It leads out of trying to become worthy by pain.

And it leads into something far better:

- the relief of truth

- the warmth of the Father

- the restoration of identity

- the peace of right direction

- the beginning of life again

This is why the father did not say,
"My son has finally improved."

He said,
"My son was dead, and is alive again."

That is the language of the Kingdom.

God is not just trying to make bad people behave better.
He is bringing dead places back to life.

He is restoring what was lost.
He is reordering what was misdirected.
He is calling people out of dead works and into living union
In Christ.

That is why repentance is not the end of the chapter.

It is the doorway.

6. The Real Shift: From Self-Salvation to Receiving Life

At its core, striving is often an attempt at self-salvation.

It may not call itself that.
It may wear spiritual language.
It may sound noble.
It may even be applauded by religious systems.

But underneath it often sits the same old lie:

"If I do enough, I can secure my own peace."

That is the ancient path.

It is the path of self-covering.
The path of self-justifying.
The path of reaching for life apart from trust.

But repentance breaks that cycle.

Repentance says:

- I cannot create life by effort.

- I cannot heal condemnation with more condemnation.

- I cannot outrun dead works by becoming better at them.

- I cannot manufacture what can only be received from God.

This is where the heart begins to soften. This is where the soul stops bargaining. This is where the person finally becomes available to grace.

And grace is not weakness.

Grace is the power of God's love meeting a turned heart.

Grace is what lifts a man out of the pigpen without first requiring him to become clean enough to be carried.

Grace is what puts the robe on before the resume is read.

Grace is what says:

Turn—and I will meet you in the road.

That is the beginning of life.

7. From Striving to Life Is the First Breath of Freedom

There is a feeling many people know well:

The tightness of striving.
The pressure to fix everything.
The fear of not measuring up.
The heaviness of internal accusation.
The endless effort to become acceptable.

And then there is another feeling.

The first breath after surrender.
The quiet relief of truth.
The deep exhale of being received.
The strange peace that comes when you stop defending yourself.
The warmth of realizing the Father is not resisting your return.

That is what repentance should begin to feel like.

Not terror.
Not endless groveling.
Not religious performance.

But the first breath of freedom.

Not freedom to wander—
freedom to return.

Not freedom to drift—
freedom to live.

Not freedom from responsibility—
freedom from the dead system that convinced you life could
be earned through pain.

This is why repentance from dead works is the first doctrine.

Because until this shift happens, every other doctrine can be
misunderstood through the lens of striving.

But once a person begins to see the Father rightly,
the whole path begins to open.

Dead works keep a person busy,
but they cannot make him alive.

The prodigal son did not come home by earning.
He came home by turning.

And when he turned, the father did not offer wages.
He offered restoration.

That is the shift from striving to life.

Repentance is not the loss of your worth.
It is the return to your true source.

It is the end of trying to save yourself
and the beginning of receiving life from God.

Repentance from dead works is not God pushing you down. It is God opening the door back into life In Christ.

Guided Direction

1. **When you feel distance from God, do you instinctively move toward relationship—or toward performance?**
   If your first reflex is to "do more" so you can feel worthy again, you may still be trying to earn what can only be received through God's love.

2. **Are you trying to become acceptable by effort, usefulness, or spiritual activity?**
   Dead works often hide inside sincere effort. If your peace rises and falls with your performance, striving may still be acting as your source.

3. **Do you secretly believe pain, pressure, or self-punishment makes you more spiritual?**
   Many people mistake heaviness for holiness. But the Father restores sons, not hired servants trying to buy their way back.

4. **What would change in your inner world if you truly believed repentance leads home, not rejection?**
   If repentance became a return instead of a threat, your soul would begin to relax, your heart would soften, and life would become possible again.

5. **Where is God inviting you today: to work harder for life—or to turn and receive it?**
   The path into freedom is not usually found in more strain. It is often found in a clearer turn toward the Father, through the Son, into life **In Christ**.

Striving says, "Become worthy, then come."
The Father says, "Come—and I will restore what striving could never build."

SECTION 5 — WHAT DIRECTION ARE YOU REALLY FACING?

This is where repentance becomes real.

Core Scripture

"And he said unto them, Why call ye me, Lord, Lord, and do not the things which I say?"
— *Luke 6:46 (KJV)*

There comes a point in every spiritual journey where the question is no longer, *What do I believe?*
The question becomes, *What direction am I actually moving in?*

Not when a person feels bad.
Not when a person makes a promise.
Not even when a person agrees with the truth.

Repentance becomes real when direction changes.

A man can speak the right language and still walk the wrong road.
He can know the scriptures and still be ruled by fear.
He can call Jesus "Lord" and still let the soul make the final decision.

That is why the Doctrine of Christ is not merely information.
It is direction.

And this first foundation stone does not only ask what you know.
It asks what you are facing.

1. Repentance Is Proven by Direction, Not Emotion

Many people mistake emotion for transformation.

They think that because they felt convicted, they have changed.
Because they cried, they have turned.
Because they were moved in a moment, they have entered a new way of life.

But emotion can be real while direction remains unchanged.

A man can weep over the pain of his life and still return to the same pattern tomorrow.
He can hate the fruit while still protecting the root.
He can feel sorrow for the outcome while still face the same old road.

That is why repentance must become more than a feeling.

It must become a reorientation of the whole person.

The body must stop running toward what is killing it.
The soul must stop defending what keeps it trapped.
And the spirit must begin to wake to the call of **God's love**.

Because to live **In Christ** is not merely to admire a better direction.

It is to turn and begin walking in it.

Repentance is not proved by intensity. It is proved by trajectory.

2. The Prodigal Son Did Not Just Feel Lost—He Faced Home

The prodigal son remains the clearest mirror in this chapter because he shows us what repentance actually looks like.

He had already suffered.
He had already fallen.
He had already discovered that the road he chose did not lead to life.

But the breakthrough did not happen when he became hungry.

It happened when he *came to himself.*

That phrase carries enormous weight.

He was not becoming someone new in that moment.
He was finally waking up to what was true.

He saw where he was.
He saw what his choices had produced.
He saw that even the servants in his father's house lived under better covering than the freedom he had chosen.

And then he did the simplest, most powerful thing:

He turned.

Not perfectly.
Not with a polished speech.
Not with full understanding.

He simply faced home.

That is repentance.

The son's journey back was not powered by self-confidence.
It was powered by the faint but living memory that there
was still goodness in the father's house.

And that is how many people begin.

Not with full theology.
Not with strong discipline.
Not with spiritual maturity.

But with a dawning awareness that **God's love** is better
than the life they are currently feeding.

The son's feet moved because his direction changed.

And once he faced the father, the father ran to meet him.

That is the mercy hidden inside repentance.

When a man turns toward life **In Christ**, he does not walk
alone for long.

3. You Can Be Near the Right Things and Still Face the Wrong Way

This is where the chapter gets honest.

Because many people are closer to the things of God than
the prodigal son was—and yet they are still not facing home.

You can attend church and still be facing performance.
You can read the Bible and still be facing fear.
You can pray and still be facing self-preservation.
You can serve and still be facing approval.
You can say all the right words and still be building your life around condemnation.

That is why Jesus said,
"Why call ye me, Lord, Lord, and do not the things which I say?"

He was not rejecting confession.
He was exposing contradiction.

A mouth can point one way while a life points another.

This is not written to shame the reader.
It is written to free them.

Because once you can see what direction you are really facing, you can finally stop pretending.

And that is mercy.

A false image keeps a man trapped.
Truth gives him somewhere to stand.

Many believers have spent years around spiritual language while their inner life still faces survival, striving, resentment, hidden fear, or self-rule.

They are near the right things, but their heart is still pointed toward the old country.

This is why the Doctrine of Christ matters.

It does not merely ask, Do you agree with the truth?
It asks, What are you becoming by the direction you keep choosing?

4. Direction Is Revealed by What You Repeatedly Return To

If you want to know what direction you are really facing, do not begin with your intentions.

Begin with your patterns.

Intentions can sound holy.
Patterns tell the truth.

When pressure rises, where do you turn?

When fear appears, what do you trust?
When disappointment hits, what story do you repeat?
When temptation speaks, what voice gets the final say?
When silence comes, what fills the space?

These are not small questions.

They reveal direction.

Because direction is not discovered in your strongest five minutes.
It is revealed in your repeated reflex.

If the body always runs to appetite, that tells you something.
If the soul always runs to old pain, that tells you something.
If the mind always returns to condemnation, that tells you something.
If your inner life keeps turning toward control instead of surrender, that tells you something.

But if, even imperfectly, you are learning to return to truth...
If you are learning to pause...
If you are learning to remember the Father's house...
If you are learning to let **God's love** interrupt the old loop...
If you are learning to bring the body, soul, and spirit back under the direction of Christ...

Then something beautiful is happening.

You are turning.

And that turn, repeated over time, becomes a path.
That path, walked long enough, becomes a life.
And that life is the beginning of learning to live **In Christ**.

You do not need perfection to know your direction. You
need honesty.

5. The First Foundation Stone Ends With a Mirror

This chapter began by exposing dead works and the cycle of
striving.

It showed the younger son leaving home.
It followed him into famine, emptiness, and awakening.
It brought that pattern into the reader's own life.
It showed the shift from striving to life.

And now it ends where all real repentance must end:

With a mirror.

Not a mirror of shame.
A mirror of direction.

What are you facing when no one is watching?
What do you return to when life gets hard?
What path are your habits strengthening?
What voice are you following when your soul gets loud?
What road are your daily choices quietly building?

These questions are not here to trap you.

They are here to reveal the road beneath your feet.

Because if you can see the road, you can change direction.

And if you can change direction, you can begin again.

This is the mercy of the Father.

He does not require you to have already arrived.
He calls you to turn.

He does not ask for a polished speech.
He asks for an honest heart.

He does not begin the Doctrine of Christ with spiritual performance.

He begins with repentance.

A turn.
A reorientation.
A new facing.

And from that moment forward, the whole journey opens.

Repentance asks one simple question: not what do you say—but what way are you truly facing?

Guided Reflection

1. When pressure rises, what direction does your life naturally turn?

- Do you turn toward prayer, truth, and the quiet strength of **God's love**?

- Or do you turn toward control, fear, escape, or old habits of self-protection?

- In other words, when life tightens, does your reflex move you closer to life **In Christ**—or back toward survival?

Your first reflex may not define your destiny, but it does reveal your current training.

2. What repeated pattern is most honestly revealing your direction right now?

- What do you repeatedly return to when you feel weak, disappointed, lonely, frustrated, or tempted?

- What story does your soul keep replaying?

- What appetite, fear, or familiar comfort keeps pulling your body and mind back into the same cycle?

Your repeated return usually tells the truth more clearly than your best intentions.

3. Where are you close to the things of God, but not yet fully facing Him?

- Are you around scripture, prayer, or church life, yet still driven by guilt, performance, fear, or approval?

- Are you speaking the language of faith while still leaning on self-effort?

- Are you near the Father's house, but inwardly still pointed toward the old country?

This is not failure.
This is clarity.
And clarity is often the first mercy of repentance.

4. If someone watched your daily habits, what direction would they say you are facing?

- Would they see a life moving toward surrender, peace, trust, and increasing alignment **In Christ**?

- Or would they see a life still shaped by hurry, pressure, control, resentment, appetite, or inner unrest?

- Would they say your habits are strengthening life—or strengthening the road you say you want to leave?

Sometimes the clearest mirror is the one that steps outside your own explanation.

5. What one honest turn would prove a new direction this week?

- What would it look like for your body, soul, and spirit to face home again in one practical way?

- What one choice would move you out of striving and into trust?

- What one act would prove—not just emotionally, but directionally—that you are turning toward life in the Father's house?

The next step does not need to be dramatic.
It just needs to be real.

Reinforcement Line

Repentance is not merely sorrow for the road behind you—it is the honest turn that proves you are now facing life In Christ.

From Turning Away to Turning Toward

Repentance from dead works is not the end of the journey.
It is the beginning of clear direction.

Many people have been taught repentance as if it means living forever with their head turned backward—replaying mistakes, grieving failures, and trying to prove they are no longer the person they once were. But that is not the path into life. That is just another form of bondage dressed in religious language.

True repentance is not a life of staring at what was behind you.
It is the moment you turn because something better has become visible.

That is why repentance from dead works must be understood as the first directional shift into life *In Christ*. It is the moment the soul stops circling the same empty places. It is the moment the body is no longer being driven by appetite alone. It is the moment the spirit begins to wake to a different source of life.

You are not being called to spend your life proving you left the pigpen.
You are being called to walk toward the Father's house.

That is the beauty of the first foundation stone in the Doctrine of Christ.

Repentance is not merely sorrow over what was lost.
It is a Spirit-led reorientation toward what is alive.

And hidden inside that turn is **Grace.**

Grace is what makes repentance possible.
Grace is what lets a man see home while he is still in the far country.
Grace is what gives him the courage to rise.
Grace is what meets him before he has the words to explain himself.

Before the son could make a case, the Father was already watching.
Before he could finish his speech, the Father was already running.
Before he could earn his place back, love had already moved.

That is the pattern.

Repentance is the turn.
Grace is the welcome.
And together, they open the path into life *In Christ*.

But turning away from dead works is only half of the movement.

If repentance tells us what we are leaving, the next question becomes unavoidable:

What are we turning toward?

If the old direction was self-effort, fear, appetite, shame, control, and condemnation...
what is the new direction?
If dead works cannot give life...
where does life actually come from?
If the soul is no longer meant to steer by pain, memory, or survival...
what is now meant to become its true reference point?

This is where the second foundation stone becomes essential.

Because once a person turns, they need somewhere true to place their weight.

Not in themselves.
Not in their feelings.
Not in religious performance.
Not in the unstable support systems of the world.

They need a source.

They need a support strong enough to hold body, soul, and spirit.
They need a direction strong enough to keep them moving when old patterns call them back.
They need something more than a decision.
They need someone trustworthy.

This is why the Doctrine of Christ does not stop at repentance from dead works.
It moves immediately into **faith toward God**.

Because repentance changes your direction...
but faith determines what now holds your life.

Repentance says, *I can no longer live from what is killing me.*
Faith says, *I now turn toward the One who is life.*

Repentance breaks the old agreement.
Faith establishes the new alignment.

Repentance loosens your grip on the false supports.
Faith teaches you where to stand. And this is where many believers have struggled without realizing it.

They have turned away from obvious sin.
They have turned away from destructive cycles.
They have even turned away from some forms of dead religion.

But they have not yet learned how to anchor their lives toward God as the true source of support.

So they turn...
but then drift.

They stop one behavior...
but remain inwardly ungrounded.

They leave Egypt...
but do not yet know how to live under the cloud.

That is why Chapter 2 matters so deeply.

Because the Christian life was never meant to be built on human strain, emotional volatility, or spiritual guesswork.

It was always meant to be built on a growing recognition that **He is**.

That God is not merely an idea to agree with.
Not merely a doctrine to defend.
Not merely a name attached to our beliefs.

He is the living source.

He is the One toward whom the whole life must now lean.

And until body, soul, and spirit begin to recognize Him as their true support, the old instinct to self-carry will keep trying to rebuild what repentance already tore down.

So Chapter 1 has brought us to the turn in the road.

Now Chapter 2 asks the deeper question:

What kind of life becomes possible when your whole being begins to trust God as the true source of support?

That is where we go next.

Not merely away from death—
but toward life.

Not merely out of dead works—
but into living trust.

Not merely into better behavior—
but into a new foundation.

Because to live *In Christ* is not simply to stop doing what
destroys you.

**To live In Christ is to flow in the anointed presence
of God's love like Jesus.**

And that kind of life must be built on faith toward God.

**Repentance turns you from what cannot carry you.
Faith toward God teaches you where life truly rests.**

CHAPTER 2 — FAITH TOWARD GOD

Faith That Knows Where to Lean

Chapter Core Scripture

"But without faith it is impossible to please him: for he that cometh to God must believe that he is, and that he is a rewarder of them that diligently seek him."
— Hebrews 11:6 (KJV)

Faith is one of the most familiar words in the Christian life—and yet, one of the least understood.

Many people say they believe in God.
Many people speak the language of faith.
But when pressure rises, their inner world often leans somewhere else.

Peace disappears when outcomes change.
Confidence fades when circumstances shift.
Decisions become driven by fear, control, or uncertainty.

This is not a failure of belief.
It is a question of support.

At its simplest, **faith is a confident expectation**.

But faith toward God is not just confidence in something—it is **a confident expectation in God's love**.

That is the shift this chapter is built around.

Because every person already lives by faith.
Every person already leans on something.

The real question is not, *"Do you have faith?"*
The real question is, *"What is your faith resting on?"*

And that is why Scripture says it is **impossible** to please
God without faith.

Not because God is difficult to please...
...but because without a confident expectation in His love,
the heart will always lean on something lesser.

This chapter is not about trying harder to believe.

It is about learning where to lean.

It is about moving from unstable supports into a life
anchored *In Christ*—where the body, soul, and spirit begin
to rest in the Father as their true source.

Here, faith moves from something we say...
to something that quietly carries us.

Chapter Flow — The Movement of Faith Toward God

1. The Crisis of Unsupported Living

Why people still feel unstable, anxious, and driven even
while claiming belief.
This section exposes the real issue: not lack of belief, but
misplaced support. It reveals how the body and soul
continue leaning on fear, control, people, money, and
outcomes—even while professing faith.

2. Coming to God as He Truly Is

Faith begins with recognizing that God *is*—not as imagined,
but as revealed.
Here, faith is grounded in reality, not wishful thinking. We
begin to see God as He has made Himself known, and faith
becomes a response to truth rather than an effort to create
it.

3. What Are You Leaning On Right Now?

Bringing faith into personal clarity.
This section draws the reader inward, helping them
recognize where their trust is actually resting—across body,
soul, and spirit. Not what they say they believe, but what is
truly carrying their reactions, decisions, and peace.

4. From Inner Strain to Anchored Trust

The turning point from pressure to rest.
Here the shift begins. Faith becomes lived, not just defined.
The strain of self-reliance starts to give way to a deeper trust
in God's love, and the inner life begins to stabilize.

5. Who—or What—is Holding You Up?

The final question beneath all faith.
This section sharpens the entire chapter into one clear
direction: identifying the true source of support. Because
whatever holds you up... ultimately shapes your life.

Before faith can become anchored, something must first be
seen clearly.

Many lives feel unstable—not because God is absent...
but because the weight of life is being carried by something
that cannot hold it.

So we begin where every good foundation begins:

Not with what you say you believe...
but with what is actually holding you up.

SECTION 1 —THE CRISIS OF UNSUPPORTED LIVING

Why is it impossible to please God without faith...?

Core Scripture

*"But without faith it is impossible to please him:
for he that cometh to God must believe that he is,
and that he is a rewarder of them that diligently
seek him."*
— Hebrews 11:6 (KJV)

Why would Scripture say something so strong?

Not difficult.
Not uncommon.
Not rare.

Impossible.

Why is it *impossible* to please God without faith?

Because without faith, the human heart will always lean on something else.

And whatever we lean on most... shapes us most.

That is why this doctrine matters so deeply.

1. Faith Is Not First a Religious Word

Faith is often spoken about as if it only belongs in church.

But faith is not first a religious word.
It is a human reality.

At its simplest, faith is a confident expectation.

Every person lives by it.
Every person leans by it.
Every person wakes up each day with some inner expectation about what life is, what people are, what tomorrow may bring, and what is worth trusting.

Some have faith in money.
Some have faith in routines.
Some have faith in their own strength.
Some have faith in relationships.
Some have faith in systems.
Some have faith in luck.
Some have faith in their fears more than they realize.

So the issue is not whether a person has faith.

The issue is: what direction is that faith facing?

That is why Hebrews does not merely say *faith*.

It says faith toward God.

This is not just confidence.
This is directional confidence.

This is relational confidence.

This is not merely a confident expectation that *something* will work out.

This is a confident expectation in God's love.

That is the shift.

And that is why this second foundation follows repentance so perfectly.

Repentance from dead works turns us away from unsupported striving.
Faith toward God turns us toward true support.

One is the turn away.
The other is the **turn toward**.

Without that second movement, a person may stop running in circles… but still not know where to stand.

2. The Real Crisis Is Not Lack of Effort, But Wrong Support

Throughout life, the body, soul, and spirit are constantly looking for support.

The body looks for safety, comfort, relief, and provision.

The soul looks for meaning, approval, control, reassurance, and emotional stability.

The spirit was made to live from something deeper still —
from the unseen reality of God's love, from the Father as
source, from life *In Christ*.

But if the spirit is not awake and aligned, the soul takes
over.

And when the soul takes over, it does what it has always
done:

It leans on what it can see.
It leans on what it can predict.
It leans on what it can control.
It leans on what has worked before.
It leans on what promises quick relief.

That is where unsupported living begins.

It often looks normal.
It often looks wise.
It can even look spiritual.

But beneath the surface, the whole inner life is being held up
by temporary things.

Money becomes support.
People become support.
Success becomes support.
Routine becomes support.
Comfort becomes support.
Health becomes support.
Control becomes support.
Even ministry can become support if it replaces the Father.

And when those things shake, the person shakes with them.

Not because they are weak.
Not because they are fake.

But because they are drawing stability from what was never meant to carry the full weight of a human life.

That is the crisis of unsupported living.

3. Scripture Repeats the Pattern Again and Again

Scripture is full of men and women who had to discover this the hard way.

Abraham had to leave what was familiar before he could learn what it meant to trust what was unseen.

Moses had to discover that zeal without God's direction could not produce God's outcome.

David had to strengthen himself in the Lord when every visible support around him was collapsing.

The woman with the issue of blood had exhausted every earthly option before reaching toward something greater.

Again and again, the pattern is the same:

Visible supports fail.
Human strength reaches its limit.
God's love reveals a deeper foundation.
Faith becomes the bridge between collapse and restoration.

Even Peter — though we will come back to him more fully in the next section — shows how quickly a man can rise in confidence, sink in fear, fail in weakness, and yet still be restored by Christ.

This is why faith is not first about performance.

It is about support.

It is about what your body trusts when it feels threatened.

It is about what your soul leans on when it feels unstable.

It is about whether your spirit turns toward God... or only remembers Him when everything else has already failed.

4. Faith and Hope Are Not the Same Thing

This revelation matters because many people confuse **faith** with **hope**, and the confusion keeps them unstable.

Faith is a confident expectation.
Hope is the anticipation of a future good / future pleasure.

Hope looks forward.
Faith leans now.

Hope says, I long for what may come.
Faith says, I know what I am standing on.

Both matter.

But if hope is not anchored in true faith, it becomes wishful thinking.

And if faith is not turned toward God, it becomes confidence in something lesser.

That is why Hebrews 11:6 is so sharp.

Without a confident expectation in God's love, it is impossible to please God.

Why?

Because without that confidence, the soul will keep building on other foundations.

And whatever we trust most... supports us most.
And whatever supports us most... shapes us most.

5. This Doctrine Is a Diagnosis Before It Becomes a Direction

This is where many believers quietly live.

They love God in principle, but in practice they still lean on lesser supports.

They speak the language of faith, but the structure underneath is still built on human reinforcement.

So when outcomes change, they lose peace.

When finances tighten, they lose confidence.

When people disappoint them, they lose direction.

When the body hurts, they lose momentum.

When prayers seem delayed, they lose heart.

When emotions turn dark, they begin questioning what they thought they believed.

This is not condemnation.

This is diagnosis.

A good builder does not hate the house because the wall is cracking.

He finds out what is not carrying the weight.

That is what this doctrine does. It does not shame the reader. It reveals the support problem.

And that revelation matters, because once the real issue is seen, the direction becomes clear.

Repentance says:

I cannot keep living from what is killing me.

Faith toward God says:

I will now lean where life actually is.

To live *In Christ* is to flow in the anointed presence of **God's love** like Jesus.

That means faith toward God is not merely believing God exists.

It is learning to let the weight of your life rest on the Father as your true source.

Before the answer arrives...
Before the feeling changes...
Before the outcome becomes visible...
Before the soul settles down...

He is.

That is where faith begins.

Not in certainty about every detail.
Not in emotional calm.
Not in perfect understanding.

But in the settled turning of the heart toward the One who is.

Guided Discovery

1. When pressure rises, do you first reach for control, comfort, money, people, or visible outcomes — or is your heart learning to turn toward the Father first?
If your first instinct is still visible reinforcement, that is usually where unsupported living is hiding. If your heart is beginning to turn toward the Father before the outcome changes, faith toward God is already beginning to form.

2. Are you mostly hoping things will improve, or are you learning to stand in a confident expectation of God's love before relief arrives?
If you are only longing for future change, that is hope looking ahead. If you are already leaning on the Father now, even before the answer appears, that is faith toward God.

3. If the visible supports in your life were shaken today, would your inner world collapse with them — or would something deeper still remain?
If everything falls with what can be seen, the foundation is still too shallow. But if something deeper remains — even while you feel the shaking — that is evidence that God is becoming your true support *In Christ*.

Closing Reinforcement

"Trust in the LORD with all thine heart; and lean not unto thine own understanding."
— Proverbs 3:5 (KJV)

Faith toward God is the slow, holy retraining of the inner life.

It is the moment the soul stops demanding that visible things carry invisible weight.

It is the beginning of learning where to lean.

Bridge to Section 2

And nowhere is this seen more clearly than in a man who loved Jesus, stepped out in boldness, sank in fear, failed in public, and still came back.

In the next section, we move from the doctrine... to the man.

From the principle... to Peter.

SECTION 2 — THE MAN WHO SANK AND STILL CAME BACK

There is something about Peter that makes him hard to forget.

Core Scripture:
"And immediately Jesus stretched forth his hand, and caught him..." — *Matthew 14:31 (KJV)*

"But without faith it is impossible to please him: for he that cometh to God must believe that he is..."
— Hebrews 11:6 (KJV)

He was bold before he was stable.
Loyal before he was mature.
Willing before he was anchored.

Peter was the kind of man who could step out of the boat
one moment... and sink in the next. And that is exactly why
he matters here.

Because **faith toward God** is not first revealed in a man
who never trembled.
It is revealed in a man who **left the boat, lost focus,
cried out, and was still caught**.

Peter is not the witness of perfect faith.
Peter is the witness of **returning faith**.

He is the man who sank...
and still came back.

And for many people, that is where this chapter begins.

Not with a polished theology.
Not with a life that looks steady from the outside.
But with the honest realization that somewhere between
wanting Jesus and walking with Him...
they started sinking under the weight of what they saw.

That is where faith toward God becomes more than a
phrase.

That is where it becomes survival.
That is where it becomes direction.
That is where it becomes the difference between panic and
peace.

Because faith is not merely believing that God exists
somewhere in the background of your life.
Faith toward God is the turning of the whole inner man
toward the One who is actually able to hold you up.

And Peter shows us what that looks like in motion.

1. Peter Did Not Fail Because He Left the Boat

When Jesus came to the disciples walking on the sea, the moment itself was already beyond reason.

The wind was against them.
The water was unstable.
The night was dark.
And what they saw did not fit their understanding.

Peter, being Peter, did what Peter does.

He spoke first.
He moved first.
He tested the moment with all the fire of a man who would rather fail moving toward Jesus than stay safe without Him.

"Lord, if it be thou, bid me come unto thee on the water." — Matthew 14:28 (KJV)

Jesus answered with one word:

"Come."

And Peter stepped out. That matters. Because many people read this story and remember Peter sinking.
But heaven first recorded Peter **coming**.

He got out of the boat.

The others stayed where they were.
Peter moved toward Christ.

He did not fail because he left the boat.
He failed because he let what was under him and around him become bigger than the One who called him.

That is the first great lesson of faith toward God.

The problem is not always that people are trying too much. Sometimes the problem is that once they begin, they stop relating to God as the truest thing in the moment.

They begin in faith…
and then shift back into sight.

They start in response…
and then return to reaction.

They move because Jesus said *"Come"*…
but halfway there, the wind becomes louder than the Word.

And that is where many souls live.

They took a few steps once.
They once believed.
They once felt the pull of God's love.
They once moved with conviction.
But when the pressure increased, the old supports rushed back in.

Fear.
Logic.
Control.
Self-protection.
People's opinions.
Money.
Outcomes.
Past pain.

And suddenly the water feels more real than the voice of Christ. That is not just Peter's story.

That is the story of almost everyone who has ever tried to walk toward God while still learning what it means to trust Him.

2. The Moment Peter Sank, He Became More Honest Than Most Religious People

Peter walked on water.

Even if only for a moment, he did what no human logic could sustain. Then he saw the wind.
He felt the instability.
His attention shifted from Christ to circumstance.

And then came one of the most human verses in all of Scripture:

"But when he saw the wind boisterous, he was afraid; and beginning to sink, he cried, saying, Lord, save me." — *Matthew 14:30 (KJV)*

Beginning to sink.

Not instantly gone.
Not fully under.
Not dead.

Just... sinking.

That is a powerful phrase.

Because many people are not in full collapse.
They are in the far more deceptive place of **beginning to sink**.

Still smiling.
Still posting.
Still functioning.
Still saying the right words.
Still calling themselves believers.

But inwardly?

Their peace is slipping.
Their reactions are unstable.
Their body is tense.
Their soul is overworking.
Their mind is rehearsing outcomes.
Their heart is tired.

They are beginning to sink. And here is what makes Peter so important: he cried out immediately.

He did not pretend.
He did not posture.
He did not quote something to impress the other disciples.
He did not protect his image.

He told the truth in the shortest prayer possible:

"Lord, save me."

That may be one of the purest acts of faith in the whole story. Because faith toward God is not always loud confidence. Sometimes it is the refusal to hide your need from the One who can actually help.

Sometimes faith is not *"I've got this."*
Sometimes faith is:

"I do not have this... but You do."

That is not weakness.
That is alignment.

That is a soul turning toward reality. And if we are honest, this is where many people first truly come to God.

Not when life is calm.
Not when they feel spiritual.
Not when the sermon lands just right.

But when the soul runs out of false supports.

When the inner scaffolding starts shaking.
When the body is tired.
When the mind is loud.
When the heart cannot carry itself anymore.

That is often when a person stops performing belief...
and starts reaching for God.

3. Jesus Did Not Shame Him—He Caught Him

This is where the whole chapter starts to glow.

Peter cried out. And Jesus did not lecture him from a distance.

He did not say,
"Why did you get out of the boat?"
He did not say,
"You embarrassed yourself in front of everyone."
He did not say,
"Come back when your faith is stronger."

Scripture says:

"And immediately Jesus stretched forth his hand, and caught him..." — *Matthew 14:31 (KJV)*

Immediately.

That word matters.

Jesus did not hesitate.
He did not make Peter earn rescue.
He did not wait for Peter to prove sincerity.

He reached.

This is why **faith toward God** must be rooted in who God truly is. Because many people still imagine God through the lens of religion, fear, disappointment, or their own earthly authority figures.

They think:

- God is distant

- God is irritated

- God is waiting for them to get it right first

- God is measuring performance before giving support

- God helps the strong, not the sinking

But Peter's story destroys that lie.

Jesus did not respond to Peter's weakness with rejection. He responded with presence. He responded with immediate support.

This is why Hebrews says:

"He that cometh to God must believe that he is..." — *Hebrews 11:6 (KJV)*

Not merely that He exists.

But that **He is**.

He is what?

He is who He reveals Himself to be.

And throughout Scripture, God reveals His heart most clearly in the pattern Peter experienced:

- near, not distant

- responsive, not indifferent

- truthful, not flattering

- holy, but not cruel

- strong enough to rescue

- loving enough to receive

And when God declared His own nature to Moses, He said:

"The Lord, The Lord God, merciful and gracious, longsuffering, and abundant in goodness and truth..." — Exodus 34:6 (KJV)

That is the God Peter cried to.

That is the God faith must turn toward.

Not a religious projection.
Not a fearful caricature.
Not the god of condemnation.

The true God.

The One whose strength does not disappear when yours does.

The One whose hand still moves when your footing fails.

4. Peter Sank More Than Once—But He Kept Returning

If the water scene were Peter's only failure, it would already be enough.

But Peter's witness goes deeper.

Because later, Peter did not just sink in fear.

He denied Jesus.

Three times.

The same man who said,
"Though all men shall be offended because of thee, yet will I never be offended,"
became the man warming himself near another fire, saying,
"I know not the man."

That is not just instability.
That is heartbreak.

That is the collapse of self-confidence.
That is the destruction of self-image.
That is the shattering of the version of yourself you thought was strongest.

And yet...

Peter still came back.

That is why he is the right witness for this chapter.

Because faith toward God is not proven by never failing.
It is proven by where you turn after you fail.

Peter wept bitterly.
But he did not stay gone.

Peter returned to the shoreline.
Peter heard his name in restoration.
Peter stood in the firelight of grace.
Peter was asked three times if he loved the One he had
denied.

And Jesus did not merely forgive him.

He recommissioned him.

"Feed my sheep."

That is staggering.

The man who could not hold himself up...
became a man who would strengthen others.

The man who sank...
became a stone.

Not because Peter became naturally strong. But because he
kept turning toward the One who was.

This is one of the deepest truths in this chapter:

Faith toward God is not the absence of weakness.
It is the repeated return of the heart to the true source of
support.

That is where many readers need permission to breathe.

You may have sunk before.
You may have panicked.
You may have denied what you once said you believed.
You may have returned to fear, control, self-protection, or
striving.

But if you are still turning back toward Him... You are not
disqualified. You are still in the story.

5. Faith Begins When God Becomes More Real Than What You Fear

Peter's life gives us a picture more powerful than theory.

He was unstable.
He was emotional.
He was impulsive.
He was sincere.
He was flawed.
He was brave.
He was inconsistent.

In other words…

He was human.

And yet Jesus chose him. Not because Peter was already finished.
But because Peter was willing to keep turning.

This is why faith toward God must be taught as more than religious agreement.

Faith is not merely:

- believing doctrines in your head

- attending meetings

- saying the right phrases

- admiring Jesus from the boat

Faith begins when the inner man starts to recognize:

God is more real than the storm.
God is more dependable than the supports I built.
God's love is more stable than my reactions.

And life In Christ is stronger than the panic I feel in the moment.

That is where faith starts becoming directional.

That is where the body begins to calm.
That is where the soul stops scrambling for counterfeit support.
That is where the spirit begins to wake up and face the Father again.

Not perfectly. But truly. And that is enough to begin.
Because Peter's witness does not say:

"Real faith never sinks."

Peter's witness says:

"Real faith keeps turning back to the hand that catches."

Guided Discovery

Take a moment before moving forward—the key is found in the reflection.

1. **When pressure rises in your life, what do you reach for first—control, panic, distraction, another person, money, overthinking... or God?**
If your first instinct is not God, that does not mean you have no faith—it may simply reveal where your soul has learned to look for support first.

2. **Are you living from the memory of one failure, or are you still willing to return like Peter did?**
Faith toward God is not built by pretending you never sank. It is built by refusing to stay turned away after you do.

3. **What would change in your inner world if you
truly believed God's hand moves faster than your
fear?**
If that became real to you, your body could soften, your soul
could stop rehearsing disaster, and your spirit could begin
leaning toward God's love again.

Closing Reinforcement

Peter did not become the rock because he never shook.
He became steady because he kept turning back to the One
who never moved.

Faith toward God begins here: not in perfect strength, but in
a real return.

Peter's story is powerful because it is not only something we
admire in Scripture.
It is something we can recognize in ourselves.

The question is no longer just whether Peter sank.

The real question is this:

What are you leaning on right now?

SECTION 3 — WHAT ARE YOU LEANING ON RIGHT NOW?

This is why many sincere believers still feel unstable.

Anchor Scripture:
"For we walk by faith, not by sight." — 2 Corinthians 5:7 (KJV)

There is a difference between what we say we believe and what we actually lean on.

A man can say he trusts God, and still spend his days being held up by money, approval, control, routine, appearance, outcomes, or fear.

A woman can sing about surrender on Sunday and still spend the rest of the week emotionally bracing against disappointment, rejection, or uncertainty.

Not because they do not love God.
Not because they are not trying.
But because under pressure, their body and soul are often still leaning somewhere else.

Faith toward God is not measured by what we say when life is calm.
It is revealed by what holds us up when life begins to shake.

And this is where the doctrine becomes deeply personal.

Because until we can see what we are really leaning on, we will keep mistaking religious language for spiritual direction.

1. What Supports You When Pressure Hits?

Every life leans on something. The question is not *if* you are leaning. The question is *what* you are leaning on.

When pressure comes, the soul looks for support quickly.
It reaches for whatever feels familiar.
Whatever has helped it survive before.
Whatever promises relief, certainty, or control.

Sometimes that support is obvious. It may be:

- money in the bank

- a person's approval

- your own ability to fix things

- constant planning

- the need to understand everything before moving

- routines that make you feel safe

- emotional withdrawal

- distraction

- productivity

- performance

Some of these things are not evil in themselves.

Money is useful.
Planning has a place.
People matter.
Routine can be healthy.

But none of them were designed to be your foundation.

They can serve your life.
They cannot safely hold your life.

That is where many people become exhausted.

They keep leaning on temporary supports and then wonder
why their soul keeps trembling.

Anything below God may assist you.
Only God can sustain you.

That is the shift.

Faith toward God begins when the soul starts to recognize
the difference between a tool and a foundation.

2. Peter Knew What It Meant to Lean on the Wrong Thing

Peter is so powerful in this chapter because he did not fail in
theory.

He failed in public.
He failed emotionally.
He failed fast.
And he failed while loving Jesus.

That is why he is so relatable.

When Peter stepped out of the boat, he did something
extraordinary.

For a moment, he was leaning on the word of Christ more
than the evidence of the storm.

That is faith.

Not perfect confidence in himself.
Not emotional calm.
Not certainty about the weather.

He simply responded to Jesus.

But then the Scripture says:

"But when he saw the wind boisterous, he was afraid..." —
Matthew 14:30 (KJV)

That is the pivot.

Peter was still on the water.
Jesus had not moved.
The word had not changed.

But Peter's attention shifted.

And when his attention shifted, his support shifted.

He began to lean on what he could *see* instead of who had
spoken.

He leaned on the storm.
He leaned on the threat.
He leaned on the evidence of danger.
He leaned on the voice of fear.

And he began to sink.

That is not just Peter's story.

That is the daily experience of many believers.

They begin with a word from God...
and then lean back into:

- visible circumstances

- old emotional reactions

- fear of loss

- fear of failure

- fear of man

- the need to control the outcome

The storm becomes louder than the voice that called them.

And yet, Peter gives us one of the most hope-filled pictures in all of Scripture:

"Lord, save me."
And immediately Jesus stretched forth His hand.

Peter sank...
but not alone.

He lost focus...
but he did not lose access.

He faltered...
but he was still reaching toward the right Person.

That is why this chapter matters so much.

Faith toward God is not about never wobbling.

It is about learning, again and again, to lean back toward the One who holds you.

The goal is not flawless performance.
The goal is a returning direction.

That is how a man grows **In Christ**.

3. The Soul Has Old Habits of Support

Most people do not realize how fast the soul grabs for support.

It happens almost automatically.

Before your spirit has even finished saying, "Lord, I trust You," the soul may already be:

- rehearsing worst-case scenarios

- planning ten backup plans

- imagining rejection

- reaching for comfort

- defending itself

- assigning blame

- trying to regain emotional control

This does not mean you have no faith.

It means your soul has been trained by repetition.

The soul learns through experience.

If fear has been repeated, it becomes familiar.
If striving has been repeated, it becomes normal.
If self-protection has been repeated, it begins to feel wise.

That is why unsupported living can continue even inside sincere Christianity.

A person may have believed in God for years, and yet their nervous system still treats money as safety...
or people as validation...
or performance as worth...
or control as peace.

This is why **faith toward God** must become more than agreement.

It must become **retraining**.

Not just:

- "I believe God exists."

But:

- "I am learning to let my body, soul, and spirit actually rest on Him."

That is a very different thing.

And it is one of the great directional shifts of life **In Christ**.

Because God's love is not merely something to admire.

God's love is support.
God's love is stability.
God's love is what the soul was starving for all along.

4. Your Reactions Reveal Your Real Foundation

Most people discover what they are leaning on by what spills out under pressure.

Pressure is a revealer.

It reveals what is underneath the polished words.
It reveals what the soul runs to first.
It reveals what your inner world believes is safest.

If your peace collapses when money shakes...
you may be leaning on money.

If your identity collapses when people pull away...
you may be leaning on approval.

If your emotions spiral when plans change...
you may be leaning on control.

If your hope disappears when progress slows...
you may be leaning on outcomes.

If your confidence rises and falls with your own
performance...
you may be leaning on self-righteousness.

Again, none of this is written to condemn. This chapter is
not a courtroom. It is a compass.

The purpose is not shame.
The purpose is clarity.

Because clarity gives you something shame never can: a new
direction. Faith toward God begins to grow the moment you
can honestly say:

"This is where I have been leaning...
and this is why I keep shaking."

That is not failure.

That is revelation.

And revelation is mercy.

It is one of the ways God's love quietly reaches into our instability and says:

**"Now you can see it.
Now we can change it."**

5. Honest Recognition Is the Beginning of Real Faith

Many people think faith starts when you feel strong.

Often, it starts when you finally become honest.

Honest about what scares you.
Honest about what controls you.
Honest about what you run to.
Honest about what you secretly trust more than God.

This is why Peter is such a gift to the Church.

He shows us that even a man called by Christ can wobble.

Even a man with courage can sink.

Even a man with love can panic.

And yet, Jesus still builds with him.

That should encourage every reader. Because the issue is not whether you have ever leaned on the wrong thing. The issue is whether you are willing to recognize it...
and turn again.

That is faith toward God in motion.

Not religious perfection.
Not emotional invincibility.
Not pretending the storm is not real.

It is this:

Choosing, in the middle of real life, to keep bringing your weight back onto God.

Again.
And again.
And again.

That is how faith is formed.

That is how the soul is retrained.

That is how a life becomes stable.

And that is how a person gradually learns to live **In Christ** —not merely admiring God's love from a distance, but actually resting in it.

Practical Reflection

Take a moment before moving forward—the key is found in the reflection.

1. **When pressure hits your life, what do you instinctively reach for first—control, planning, approval, distraction, money, performance, or God?**
   Write down 3 real examples from recent days.

2. **What area of your life currently feels the most unstable—and what might that instability be revealing about what you've been leaning on?**
   Write down 3 honest observations.

3. **If you truly believed God's love could hold you in that area, what would begin to change in your reactions this week?**
Write down 3 practical shifts you could make.

Closing Reinforcement

Peter did not sink because Jesus failed him.
He sank because, for a moment, he leaned more heavily on what he saw than on who had spoken.

Most of us have done the same.

But the mercy of God is this:

The hand of Christ is still extended toward every sinking heart.

Faith toward God is not the absence of storms.
It is the gradual retraining of the whole person to rest in the One who remains steady inside them.

And once you begin to see what you have been leaning on...
the next question becomes unavoidable:

What does it actually look like to move from unstable reaction into a life that is being held?

That is where we go next.

SECTION 5 — READY TO STEP OUT OF THE BOAT?

This is where faith becomes real.

Core Scripture:
"And Peter answered him and said, Lord, if it be thou, bid me come unto thee on the water. And he said, Come." — Matthew 14:28–29

Reinforcement Scripture:
"After this manner therefore pray ye..." — Matthew 6:9

Faith toward God is not merely believing that God exists.

It is learning to lean the weight of your life toward Him.

It is not just agreeing with truth in your mind.
It is teaching your body, your soul, your reactions, your fears, your habits, and your future to turn toward the Father as your true source.

That is where faith becomes real.

Not in the sermon.
Not in the quote.
Not in the language of belief.

But in the moment when the wind rises...
and you decide where your weight will go.

That is what Peter faced.

And that is what we face too.

So the final question of this chapter is not simply:

Do you believe in God?

The deeper question is:

Are you ready to step out of the boat?

Because there comes a moment in every life where faith
must stop being admired...
and start being practiced.

1. Faith Is Not Proven in the Boat, But in the Step

A boat feels safe because it feels familiar.

Even in a storm, there is still something under your feet that
your body understands.

And that is why so many people stay there.

Not because they hate God.
Not because they reject Jesus.
But because the boat still feels easier than trust.

For some, the boat is control.
For others, it is overthinking, planning loops, money,
people, old habits, or familiar fear.

Many people talk about faith for years while never really
leaving the boat.

But Peter did something different.

He asked for permission to move toward Jesus in the middle
of the impossible.

"Lord, if it be thou, bid me come unto thee on the water."

That is one of the most honest prayers in scripture.

He was not pretending certainty.
He was reaching for direction.

And Jesus answered with one word:

Come.

That is the invitation of this chapter.

Not understand everything first.
Not feel calm first.
Not become spiritually impressive first.

Just:

Come.

Faith toward God is not having every answer.
It is moving toward the right Person.

2. I Am Not Writing This as a Guru, But as a Fellow Traveler

I want to say something plainly here.

I am not writing this as a guru.
I am not writing this as a man who has mastered every storm, never panics, and always gets it right.

I am writing this as a fellow traveler in **God's love** and **In Christ**.

More Peter than polished.

A man who has seen enough to know the difference between chaos and support.
A man who has stumbled, learned, watched, prayed, and kept turning back toward the Father.

As a carpenter, I occasionally worked for Christian organizations.
And over time, I began to notice something I could not ignore.

In some of those places, we would see **three to five minor to major miracles a week**.

Not always dramatic in the way people imagine.
But real.

Provision arriving at the right time.
Unexpected favor.
Protection that should not have happened naturally.
Needs met.
Doors opening.
People showing up.
Solutions appearing.

Not perfect.
Not without pressure.
But there was often a very real sense of support.

Then I worked in non-Christian businesses too.

And many of those environments felt very different.

Constant chaos.
Pressure without peace.
Activity without alignment.
Everyone pushing.

Everyone reacting.
Everyone leaning on human strength alone.

That contrast stayed with me.

Not because Christians are automatically wiser.
And certainly not because every Christian workplace is
healthy.

But I saw enough to know this:

**Where people genuinely turn toward God, things
often begin to move differently.**

Not because they control God.
Not because they perform religion correctly.
But because faith honors the true source of support.

That does not remove every storm.

But it changes what holds you in one.

And that is why I am writing this chapter.

Not to stand above you.
But to stand beside you.

As a man still learning that the safest place is not always the
boat.

Sometimes the safest place is the place Jesus said,

Come.

3. If You Do Not Know How to Pray, Start Where Jesus Started

For many people, the barrier to practiced trust is not unwillingness.

It is uncertainty.

They think:

I do not know what to say.
I do not know how to pray properly.
I do not know what God expects from me.

If that is you, start with the Lord's Prayer.

Not as a ritual.
Not as a religious chant.
Not as words repeated without thought.

Jesus did not teach this prayer as ceremony.

He taught it as **relational realignment**.

When He said:

"After this manner therefore pray ye..."

He was not merely giving a script.
He was giving a pattern.

A way to bring the soul back into order.

A way to teach the inner life where support actually comes from.

Look at the movement:

Our Father...
Start with relationship.

Which art in heaven...
Lift your eyes above the storm.

Hallowed be thy name...
Realign your heart around who He is.

Thy kingdom come. Thy will be done...
Surrender outcomes before demanding them.

Give us this day our daily bread...
Ask for real provision.

Forgive us... as we forgive...
Clear the inner blockages.

Lead us not into temptation, but deliver us from evil...
Ask for guidance and protection.

This is not empty religion.

This is how a soul learns to breathe again.

This is how panic begins to loosen its grip.

This is how faith becomes practiced.

If you do not know what to pray when the wind rises, begin there.

Not because magic lives in exact wording,
but because Jesus gave us a pattern that teaches the heart
how to return to the Father.

Sometimes the most powerful prayer is not the longest one.

Sometimes it is simply:

Our Father...

And that alone can reorient an entire moment.

4. The Invitation Is Not to Be Impressive, But to Be Immersed

Faith toward God is not the end of the journey.

It is the beginning of a deeper one.

It is one thing to believe God is your source.

It is another thing to be **immersed** into a whole new pattern of life.

Peter stepping out of the boat was not just a brave moment.

It was a picture.

A man leaving one support system...
to discover another.

Leaving what felt natural...
to experience what only becomes possible through trust.

Leaving the old ground...
to learn a new way of standing.

That is why the next chapter matters so much.

Because once faith begins to turn you toward God, the next question becomes:

What are you being brought into?

Not just mentally.
Not just emotionally.
Not just doctrinally.

But fully.

Into body.
Into soul.
Into spirit.
Into pattern.
Into identity.
Into belonging.
Into a new kind of life **In Christ**.

That is why Hebrews does not say merely "baptism."

It says:

"the doctrine of baptisms."

Plural.

Because the journey into Christ is deeper than one religious event.

It is an immersion into a new reality.

5. So... Are You Ready to Step Out of the Boat?

This final question is not about becoming dramatic, strange, or emotionally intense.

It is much simpler than that.

Are you ready to begin making the Father your first direction?

Are you ready to pray before you spiral?
To ask before you assume?
To seek before you surrender to fear?
To come before you fully understand?
To trust His nature even when the outcome is not yet clear?

That is what stepping out of the boat looks like in real life.

Sometimes it is a whispered prayer.
Sometimes it is refusing to let panic make the decision.
Sometimes it is choosing not to lean on your old coping pattern.
Sometimes it is stopping the planning loop and saying:

Father, what are You saying?

That is not weak faith.

That is real faith.

And that is where this chapter lands.

Not in pressure.
Not in guilt.
Not in religious performance.

But in invitation.

Jesus is still saying:

Come.

And faith toward God is simply the grace-filled courage to answer Him.

Ready to Step Out of the Boat?

Take a moment here before moving on.

This is not about judging your past.
It is about recognizing your next step.

1. **When pressure rises, what is your usual "boat"—control, overthinking, people, money, distraction, or old habits?**
   Whatever you run to first usually reveals what still feels safest to your soul.

2. **If you do not know what to pray in hard moments, are you willing to begin with the simple pattern Jesus gave—"Our Father…"—and let that prayer realign your heart instead of becoming empty repetition?**
   Faith often begins not with eloquence, but with direction.

3. **What would it look like this week to take one real step out of the boat and toward God—before the storm gets louder?**
   Not a dramatic promise. Just one practiced movement of trust.

Section Reinforcement

Faith toward God is not learning how to stay calmer in the boat.
It is learning to trust the One who says, "Come."

Or more simply:

The boat feels familiar.
Jesus is calling you farther.

If repentance is the turning...
and faith toward God is the leaning...

Then the next movement is the **immersion**.

Because the Father never intended for you to merely admire truth from a distance.

He intends to bring you into it.

Faith turns you toward the right source.
But **baptisms** reveal the depth of what you are now being brought into.

Not just a belief.
Not just a moment.
Not just a ritual.

A life.

A new pattern.
A new identity.
A new order of support.
A deeper participation in the life of Christ.

You have turned.
You have begun to lean.
Now the question becomes:

What does it mean to be fully immersed into the life you were made for?

That is where we go next.

CHAPTER 3 — THE DOCTRINE OF BAPTISMS

God does not merely call us forward —He brings us through.

Opening Scripture
"Therefore leaving the principles of the doctrine of Christ, let us go on unto perfection... of the doctrine of baptisms..."
— Hebrews 6:1–2 (KJV)

Baptism is often reduced to a single church event, a public declaration, or a one-time act of obedience.

But Hebrews does not call it *the doctrine of baptism*. It calls it **the doctrine of baptisms**—plural. That detail matters.

It points to something deeper than one outward act. It points to the layered way God brings a person through cleansing, surrender, identification, transformation, and new life.

If repentance turns you, and faith toward God anchors you, then baptisms begin to **carry that turning and trust into your whole life**.

In real life, this doctrine shows up anywhere a person is being immersed into a pattern. Every day, people are being shaped by what they repeatedly enter—fear, pressure, grief, pleasure, culture, truth, or God's love. What surrounds you, forms you.

That is why this doctrine matters.

The doctrine of baptisms is not merely about getting wet. It is about what happens when God brings you **out of one realm and into another**—out of the old life and into a deeper life **In Christ**.

The directional shift in this chapter is from **shallow belief to full immersion**.

Many people believe in Jesus from the shoreline. They agree with truth, admire truth, and speak about truth—but have not yet allowed God to bring their body, soul, and spirit fully through the waters of change.

This chapter is about the Father's loving process of bringing what is still divided into alignment. God's love does not merely inform. It **immerses**. It surrounds. It cleanses. It buries what must die and raises what must live.

This chapter unfolds in five connected movements:

1. What Are You Really Being Immersed In?

This section defines the doctrine clearly and personally. Before we discuss biblical baptisms, we must first see that everyone is already being immersed in something. The real question is not whether you are being formed—but **what is forming you**.

2. Through the Waters: Israel, Jesus, and You

This section anchors the chapter in Scripture through the recurring pattern of passing through the waters. It shows how God uses these moments to mark transition, identity, and movement into something new.

3. Where This Immersion Is Happening in You

This section turns the mirror toward the reader. It helps reveal where the doctrine of baptisms is already showing up in your habits, reactions, patterns, and inner formation.

4. Buried, Washed, and Raised Into Life

This section explores the transforming work of baptisms—cleansing, surrender, burial, and new life. It shows how God uses immersion to move us from old patterns into life **In Christ**.

5. Have You Only Touched the Water?

This final section invites honest reflection. It asks whether you have truly passed through God's transforming work—or only stood near it without yielding to the deeper change He offers.

The doctrine of baptisms is not a side issue in Christian maturity. It is one of the Father's chosen ways of bringing a person through real change. This chapter is not asking whether you know the word *baptism*. It is asking whether you have begun to understand what God is doing when He brings a person **through the waters and into Christ**.

SECTION 1 — MORE THAN WATER

Why most people stop at the symbol and miss the immersion

Core Scripture

"Therefore leaving the principles of the doctrine of Christ, let us go on unto perfection... of the doctrine of baptisms..."
— Hebrews 6:1–2 (KJV)

Baptism is one of those words many believers think they already understand.

We hear it and immediately picture water, a public confession, a testimony, a church service, a moment we remember. None of that is wrong—but Hebrews does not say *the doctrine of baptism*. It says **the doctrine of baptisms**. Plural.

That one detail opens a much larger door than many people realize.

This section begins there, because if we reduce baptism to a single outward ceremony, we may honor the symbol while missing the deeper immersion God intended.

The doctrine of baptisms is not merely about an event to remember. It is about a pattern of transition, surrender, and formation that affects body, soul, and spirit as the Father brings a person more fully **In Christ**.

1. More Than a Ceremony

When most believers hear the word *baptism*, they think of water.

A church service.
A public confession.
A testimony.
A step of obedience.
A memory.

None of that is wrong.

But it is often incomplete.

If baptism is reduced to one outward act, then the doctrine becomes small, manageable, and easy to file away as something we already "did."

But if baptisms are a deeper pattern of God bringing a person through cleansing, surrender, identification, transformation, and new life, then this doctrine is not merely something to remember.

It is something to understand. Something to yield to. Something that continues to shape a life **In Christ**.

2. A Symbol That Carries Covenant

The doctrine of baptisms is not merely about getting wet. It is about **immersion**. It is about what happens when a person is brought fully into something until it begins to affect body, soul, and spirit.

Baptism is not only a symbol of transition—it is the pattern of being carried through transition.

It is not only the sign of identification—it is the process of being re-identified. It is not only a public witness—it is the deeper work of being surrounded by a new reality until the old life begins to lose its grip.

That is why Hebrews places this among the foundational doctrines of Christ.

Not because it is a ritual to complete,
but because it is a pattern to understand.

And one of the clearest ways to feel this is through covenant.

Baptism is as sacred as the full-immersion covenant of marriage.

3. What Is Forming You Right Now?

You can see this principle at work in everyday life. Every human being is already being immersed in something.

Some are immersed in fear until fear becomes their reflex.
Some are immersed in rejection until rejection becomes their identity.
Some are immersed in striving until performance becomes their covering.
Some are immersed in pain until pain becomes the lens through which they interpret everything.

What surrounds a person repeatedly begins to shape what comes out of them.

That is why this doctrine lands so deeply in real life.

4. What God Begins in Symbol

Israel passed through the Red Sea and left Egypt behind.
Israel passed through Jordan and entered a new land.
Jesus went into the waters of baptism and emerged into
public ministry.

The pattern is not random.

God uses passage.
God uses transition.
God uses immersion.

Again and again, He brings people through one realm and
into another.

That is the heart of this doctrine.

Repentance turns you.

Faith toward God anchors you.

But baptisms begin to **carry that turning and trust
through your whole being**.

What This May Be Revealing

The doctrine of baptisms is not here to make your faith
more complicated. It is here to make your transformation
more visible. What God begins in symbol,
He intends to complete in substance.

And in the next section, we will step into the waters of
Scripture itself and watch how God has always used passage
through the waters to mark transition, identity, and new
beginnings—from Israel, to Jordan, to Jesus, and now to
you.

SECTION 2 — JESUS WENT DOWN INTO THE WATERS

The pattern of identification, surrender, and Spirit-filled emergence

Core Scripture:
Matthew 3:13–17 (KJV)
"Then cometh Jesus from Galilee to Jordan unto John, to be baptized of him... And Jesus, when he was baptized, went up straightway out of the water: and, lo, the heavens were opened unto him, and he saw the Spirit of God descending like a dove, and lighting upon him: And lo a voice from heaven, saying, This is my beloved Son, in whom I am well pleased."

There are moments in Scripture that do more than teach a doctrine.
They reveal a pattern.

Jesus stepping down into the waters of baptism is one of those moments.

This is not just a ceremonial event placed at the beginning of His ministry because religion likes symbolic openings. This is a living picture. A doorway. A divine pattern being revealed in plain sight. Before the miracles. Before the crowds. Before the confrontations. Before the cross. Jesus goes down into the water.

And in that moment, heaven shows us something essential.

Baptism is not first about performing a ritual.
It is about identification.
It is about surrender.
It is about alignment.
It is about emergence.
It is about the life of God meeting a yielded vessel.

That is why this moment sits at the center of the chapter.

Because if repentance shows us the turn, and faith toward
God shows us what we now lean on, the doctrine of
baptisms shows us what it looks like when a person is fully
immersed into the pattern of life In Christ.

Jesus did not go into the water because He was sinful.
He went into the water because He was showing the way.

He entered the waters to identify with humanity.
He submitted to the Father's pattern.
He stepped into the place where surrender becomes visible.
And when He came up, the Spirit descended and the Father
spoke.

That is not an accident.
That is the pattern.

Baptism, in its deepest sense, is the place where heaven
witnesses a yielded life.1. Baptism Is More Than A Religious
Act

For many people, baptism has been reduced to a church
event.

A day.
A tank.
A testimony.
A photo.
A wet shirt and a handshake in the foyer.

And while there is nothing wrong with celebration, the danger is that people can walk away thinking the act itself was the whole point.

But Scripture does not treat baptism that lightly.

The doctrine of baptisms is not about one isolated religious ceremony. It is about immersion into a new reality. It is about being brought fully into the life, death, resurrection, cleansing, surrender, identity, and empowering pattern of God's love In Christ.

This is why Hebrews does not call it merely *baptism* in the singular in this foundational list. It says **"the doctrine of baptisms."**
There is depth here.
Layers here.
Movement here.

There is water baptism.
There is the baptism of the Holy Ghost.
There is the baptism into Christ's death.
There is the immersion of the whole person—body, soul, and spirit—into a new way of being.

So before we define the deeper layers, we must first see the central picture clearly.

And the clearest picture is Jesus.

Not because He needed cleansing from sin.
But because He chose to reveal the pathway of surrender.

Baptism begins where self-standing ends.

It is the visible yielding of a life to the Father's order.

It says:

I am no longer standing apart.
I am stepping into the pattern.
I am no longer preserving the old self.
I am consenting to be identified with the will of God.
I am going down so something deeper can rise.

That is why this section cannot begin with explanation alone.
It must begin with a picture.

And the picture is Jesus in the Jordan.

Baptism is not first about getting wet.
It is about yielding so deeply that heaven can witness the change in direction.

2. Jesus Entered The Waters To Reveal The Pattern

When Jesus came to John at the Jordan, even John was unsettled.

John understood enough to know something felt backward.

"I have need to be baptized of thee, and comest thou to me?" (Matthew 3:14, KJV)

In other words:

This should be the other way around.
You are the Holy One.
You are the clean One.
You are the One I have been announcing.

And yet Jesus steps forward anyway.

Why?

Because He is not entering the water as a sinner needing repentance.
He is entering the water as the Son revealing the pattern of surrender.

His answer is profound:

"Suffer it to be so now: for thus it becometh us to fulfil all righteousness." (Matthew 3:15, KJV)

Not perform religion.
Not satisfy optics.
Not create a tradition.

Fulfil all righteousness.

That means this moment is about alignment with the Father's order.

Jesus is showing us that true righteousness is not merely avoiding wrong.
It is yielding fully to the will and pattern of God.

And then the sequence unfolds.

He goes down into the water.
He identifies with the people He came to save.
He steps into humility.
He submits to the Father's timing.
He allows the act to become visible.
He rises from the water.
The heavens open.
The Spirit descends.
The Father speaks.

This is one of the clearest revealed patterns in all the Gospels.

The Pattern Revealed In The Jordan:

1. Identification
Jesus steps into the human story without standing above it.

2. Surrender
He yields to the Father's process, even when it appears
unnecessary to the natural mind.

3. Emergence
He rises from the water as heaven marks the moment.

4. Spirit Empowerment
The Spirit descends upon Him.

5. Affirmation
The Father speaks identity before public ministry begins.

That last part matters deeply.

The Father does not say,
"This is my beloved Son because He healed the sick."
"This is my beloved Son because He cast out devils."
"This is my beloved Son because He preached to
thousands."

No.

The affirmation comes **before** the public works.

Before the visible fruit.
Before the miracles.
Before the applause.
Before the rejection.

That means baptism is tied not only to surrender—but to
identity.

Jesus comes up from the water and heaven declares who He
is.

This is why the doctrine of baptisms cannot be taught as mere ritual.
It is a revealed pattern of going down in surrender so you can rise in truth.

And if we are going to live In Christ, then we are not just admiring this moment.
We are meant to recognize ourselves in it.

Jesus did not enter the waters because He needed to change.
He entered the waters to show us how yielded love steps into the Father's will.

3. Where Are You Still Standing On The Shore?

This is where the doctrine stops being theological and starts becoming personal.

Because many people admire baptism as an idea while still standing on the bank.

They believe in Jesus.
They may even love God.
They may have repented in part.
They may have begun to lean toward faith.

But there are still places in the life where they remain dry.

Still guarded.
Still self-protective.
Still preserving the old identity.
Still wanting God's blessing without God's process.
Still wanting the Spirit's power without the surrender that makes room for it.

That is the shoreline.

And the shoreline is comfortable.

You can watch others go in.
You can talk about deeper things.
You can discuss doctrine.
You can even defend truth.

But the shoreline lets you remain mostly untouched.

Baptism confronts that.

Because baptism says:

There comes a moment when agreement is no longer
enough.
There comes a moment when truth must become visible.
There comes a moment when the old stance must be
surrendered.
There comes a moment when the body, soul, and spirit must
stop negotiating and step into alignment.

This is why the doctrine of baptisms matters so much in
your life right now.

Not because God is obsessed with ceremonies.
But because God is leading you into full participation.

Some people have been baptized in water, but their soul
never went under.
Their reactions stayed the same.
Their identity stayed fragile.
Their fear stayed in charge.
Their appetites still named them.
Their history still defined them.

Others talk about the Holy Spirit, but still resist surrender.
They want power, but not process.

Experience, but not dying to self.
Comfort, but not transformation.

But the Jordan reveals something deeper.

The place of surrender is not where you lose yourself.
It is where false identity begins to break.

And for some readers, this chapter will not first be about
getting re-baptized in water.
It will be about finally recognizing where you are still
refusing immersion.

Where are you still standing back?
Where are you still editing God's process?
Where are you still trying to stay in control?
Where are you still wanting the Father to speak over a life
that has not yet yielded fully?

That is not condemnation.
That is invitation.

Because God's love does not call you into the water to shame
you.
He calls you there to free you.

**You cannot rise into the next pattern of life In
Christ while clinging to the old shoreline.**

4. The Water Is A Pattern, Not Just A Moment

Let's tighten the whole picture.

Jesus went down into the waters.
Not because He was unclean.
But because He was revealing the way.

He showed us that baptism is not first a ritual to perform.
It is a pattern to enter.

A pattern of:

- **Identification** — no longer standing apart
- **Surrender** — yielding to the Father's order
- **Alignment** — stepping into righteousness, not self-definition
- **Emergence** — rising into a visible new direction
- **Spirit Empowerment** — making room for the life of God
- **Affirmation** — receiving identity from the Father, not from performance

This is why the doctrine of baptisms belongs in the foundations of maturity.

Because without this pattern, people remain divided.

They repent, but still cling.
They believe, but still resist.
They want change, but stay on the edge.
They seek God, but preserve the old self.
They want the voice of the Father, but avoid the waters of surrender.

But Jesus shows another way.

He goes down willingly.
He comes up aligned.
The Spirit descends.
The Father speaks.

That sequence is not random.
It is revelation.

And the deeper message is this:

God's love does not merely call you to believe the pattern.
God's love calls you to enter it.

This section is not asking whether you understand baptism as a doctrine.
It is asking whether you recognize the pattern of surrender that baptism reveals.

Because the water is not the destination.

The water is the doorway.

Baptism is the visible language of a life no longer resisting God's love.

5. Are You Ready To Go Under?

Not just under water.
Under truth.
Under surrender.
Under the Father's order.
Under the life that leads deeper In Christ.

Let these questions do the work gently.

1. Are you still standing on the shoreline in an area where God is asking for surrender?

- A "yes" may look like delay, control, hesitation, or constant internal negotiation.
- A "no" means you can identify a real area where you have already stepped into obedience, even when it cost you comfort.

2. Do you want God to affirm a version of you that has not yet fully yielded?

- A "yes" often shows up as wanting peace, power, clarity, or blessing while still preserving self-rule.
- A "no" means you are beginning to understand that identity in God is received through surrender, not performance.

3. Have you treated baptism as a past event instead of a present pattern?

- A "yes" means you may have honored the act but missed the ongoing invitation to live immersed in God's love In Christ.
- A "no" means you are starting to see that baptism is not only something you once did—it is something you are still learning to live.

If these questions expose tension, that is not failure.

That is the water reaching the real places.

And that is good.

Because the Father is not trying to drown who you truly are. He is bringing the false layers to the surface so they can lose their grip.

What goes under in surrender does not come back the same.

Closing Reinforcement

Jesus in the Jordan gives us the central picture.

But the doctrine of baptisms does not stop with one moment in the water.

Because if the Jordan shows us the pattern, the rest of the New Testament shows us the depth.

There is more than one immersion at work.
More than one layer of surrender.
More than one way God brings the whole person into alignment.

And that is where we go next.

SECTION 3 — WHAT ARE YOU ACTUALLY BEING IMMERSED INTO?

Baptism is the line in the sand where one life ends and a new life In Christ begins

Core Scripture

Exodus 34:6 (KJV)
And the LORD passed by before him, and proclaimed, The LORD, The LORD God, merciful and gracious, longsuffering, and abundant in goodness and truth,

Baptism is not merely the moment a person gets wet.

It is the line in the sand.

It is the place where one life ends, and a new life **In Christ** is meant to begin.

That is why the doctrine of baptisms matters far more than most people have been taught.

Because many have crossed the line publicly...
but have never been clearly taught the life on the other side.

They entered the water.
They made the confession.
They stood before witnesses.
They felt the weight of the moment.

But after the celebration, after the towel, after the hugs, after the photos, the deeper question often remained unanswered:

What life was I actually entering?

That is the burden of this section.

Because if baptism is only taught as a symbol, many people honor the event but miss the lifestyle.

And if the new life is not accurately taught, it is rarely fully found.

This is where the doctrine of baptisms must become clear.

Not as a religious ritual.
Not as a denominational badge.
But as a public, covenantal crossing into the revealed life and nature of God's love **In Christ**.

1. Baptism, The Line in the Sand

John's baptism was not casual.

It was not decorative.
It was not merely a tradition.
It was not a photo opportunity in a river.

It was a public declaration that a person had come to a line in the sand.

They were saying:

"I can no longer keep walking the way I was walking."

"I am turning."

"I am stepping out of one direction and into another."

That is why John's baptism carried such weight.

People were not just acknowledging sin in a vague religious sense.
They were publicly admitting that the old path was not life.

They were stepping into the waters as a sign that something real had come to an end.

The old direction.
The old agreement.
The old confidence.
The old self-rule.

That is what made it powerful. And that is what many modern believers have lost.

We have often reduced baptism to a beautiful moment...

...but in Scripture, it is a threshold.

A crossing point.

A public line in the sand where one life is being left behind, and another is being embraced.

That is why it matters. Because lines matter.

A man may think long and hard before he signs a business contract.
A woman may carefully weigh a life-changing move.
A family may spend months planning a wedding because they understand that some moments divide life into *before* and *after*.

Baptism is one of those moments.

It is not small.

It is not "just a symbol."

It is a visible declaration that a person is no longer claiming the right to remain who they were.

That is serious. And it should be taught as serious.

2. Water Is the Sign—God's Nature Is the Substance

Water is the symbol. But water is not the destination.

That is where many teachings stop too early.

Yes, water speaks of cleansing.
Yes, water speaks of burial.
Yes, water speaks of washing.
Yes, water speaks of transition.

But the deeper question remains:

What is the believer actually being immersed into?

This is where Exodus 34:6 becomes profoundly important.

When the Lord passed before Moses and declared His own nature, He gave us one of the clearest revelations of who He is:

- **Merciful**
- **Gracious**
- **Longsuffering**
- **Abundant in goodness**
- **And truth**

This is not a side note in Scripture. This is the revealed flow of God's heart. This is the nature Jesus perfectly embodied. This is the life the believer is being brought into.

Baptism is not merely immersion into water.

It is a public, covenantal immersion into the revealed nature, family, and flow of God's love **In Christ**.

That means the water points beyond itself.

It points to a life immersed in:

- mercy instead of judgment
- compassion instead of indifference
- patience instead of reaction
- loving-kindness instead of hardness
- truth instead of self-deception
- forgiveness instead of resentment
- justice without cruelty

This is the "water" many believers were never clearly taught to enter.

Not just an event in a river.
Not just a tank in a church building.
Not just a moment of obedience.

A whole-life immersion into the very nature of God.

That is why this doctrine is so important.

Because if the water is understood without the nature of God, the symbol remains shallow.

But when the symbol is joined to the substance, baptism becomes alive. Then it becomes what it was always meant to be:

A crossing into the flow of God's love **In Christ**.

3. Baptism Is a Covenant of Belonging

This is why baptism should not be treated lightly.

People often spend more time preparing for marriage than they do preparing for baptism.

They think deeply about who they are joining themselves to.
They speak with family.
They seek counsel.
They celebrate the engagement.
They gather witnesses.
They make vows.
And once those vows are made, life is no longer meant to be lived as though nothing changed.

Why?

Because marriage is a public covenant of belonging.

And in spiritual significance, baptism carries that same covenantal seriousness.

It is not merely "an outward sign of an inward faith."

That statement is not entirely wrong.

It is just too thin to carry the weight of what Scripture is showing us.

Baptism is a public declaration of belonging. It is a person saying before heaven, earth, witnesses, and their own future:

"I no longer belong to the old life."

"I now identify with Christ."

"I am entering the family of God."

"I am yielding myself to the way of God's love."

"I am crossing the line, and I do not intend to live as though I never crossed it."

That is why this matters. Because covenant changes identity. And identity changes direction.

A wedding ring does not create love, but it publicly marks belonging.
A covenant does not erase all struggle overnight, but it changes what life is now meant to be built around.

So too with baptism. The believer is not just saying, "I believe something." The believer is saying, "I belong somewhere now."

That is powerful. That is serious.

And that is why baptism should echo through every remaining day of a person's life.

Not as a memory only.

As a lived reality.

4. Why Many Cross the Line but Never Find the Life

This is where the pain enters.

Because many people have sincerely been baptized ...and yet were never clearly taught what life on the other side was supposed to look like.

They crossed the line.

But no one really explained the country they had entered.

They were told to believe.
They were told to attend.
They were told to try harder.
They were told to avoid bad behavior.
They were told to "be a good Christian."

But they were not always shown the deeper pattern.

They were not clearly taught:

- how the body still pulls toward appetite
- how the soul still clings to fear, pride, offense, shame, and control
- how the spirit must be awakened and yielded
- how the life **In Christ** is not merely moral improvement, but relational immersion
- how the nature of God must become the new atmosphere of the believer's life
- how baptism points to a full-life transition, not a religious milestone

So many have honored the event...

...but never truly found the life.

Not because they were insincere.
Not because God failed them.
Not because the act meant nothing.

But because the life beyond the line was never fully taught. And what is not clearly taught is rarely deeply lived. That is why the doctrine of baptisms matters. Because if this foundation is left shallow, the believer often remains shallow.

Not fake.
Not lost beyond hope.
Just under-taught.

Still standing too close to the shoreline of the old life. Still thinking the event was the finish line... when it was meant to be the doorway.

This is one of the reasons this book matters.

Because the new life **In Christ** must be made visible enough to walk in.

5. The Baptism Lifestyle Is 100%, Not Ankle-Deep

Baptism is not calling a person to visit the waters. It is calling them to live immersed.

Not 20%.

Not 60%.

Not a spiritual mood on Sundays and a flesh-led life the rest of the week.

Not ankle-deep when convenient.
Not waist-deep when emotional.
Not shoulder-deep when surrounded by worship music.

Immersed.

Covered.

Surrounded.

Yielded.

This is the baptism lifestyle **In Christ**.

It is the life where God's love is not admired from the shoreline, but entered.

It is the life where mercy begins to reshape reactions.
Where **compassion** begins to soften instincts.
Where **patience** begins to outlast irritation.
Where **loving-kindness** begins to replace hardness.
Where **truth** becomes more important than image.
Where **forgiveness** becomes stronger than offense.
Where **justice** is no longer about revenge, but alignment with what is right in the heart of God.

This is not perfection by tomorrow. But it is full direction. It is a whole-life yes. It is the decision that the old life no longer has the right to define the new one.

That is what baptism points to.

A line in the sand.

A covenant of belonging.

A full immersion into the life and nature of God.

Practical Reflection

Take a moment before moving forward—the key is found in the reflection.

1. **When you think about your own baptism (or your desire for baptism), what did you believe it meant at the time?**
    Write down **3 honest thoughts or expectations** you had about what was beginning.

2. **Which part of God's revealed nature in Exodus 34:6 do you most sense you are being invited to live in more deeply right now— mercy, compassion, patience, goodness, truth, forgiveness, or justice?**
    Write down **3 real-life situations** where that quality needs to become more visible in you.

3. **If baptism truly marked a line in the sand for your life, what would it look like to live this week as someone who has crossed it?**
    Write down **3 practical changes** that would reflect a fuller life **In Christ**.

This is not about remembering a ceremony.

It is about entering the life the ceremony pointed to. Because baptism is not the end of the old life in theory.

It is the beginning of the new life in practice.

.

Closing Reinforcement

The waters matter.

But not because water alone changes a person.

The waters matter because they mark the place where a person says:

"The old life ends here."

And if that is true, then the next question becomes unavoidable:

What still remains above the waterline?

Because many have crossed the line...

...but parts of the old life are still resisting the immersion.

And that is where we go next.

SECTION 4 — BURIED WITH CHRIST, RAISED INTO LIFE

The deeper work of death, cleansing, and new creation

Core Scripture:
Romans 6:3–4 (KJV)
Know ye not, that so many of us as were baptized into Jesus Christ were baptized into his death? Therefore we are buried with him by baptism into death: that like as Christ was raised up from the dead by the glory of the Father, even so we also should walk in newness of life.

Baptism is not just the moment you got wet.
It is the moment heaven declares that the old direction is no longer meant to rule your life.

That is why Scripture does not speak of baptism as a light symbol alone.
It speaks of burial.
It speaks of washing.
It speaks of renewal.

It speaks of putting off the old man and walking in newness of life.

So the deeper question is not simply, **"Did you go into the water?"**

The deeper question is:

What died there?
And just as importantly:

What came back out?

1. Baptism Is a Burial Before It Is a Celebration

Many people think of baptism as a public declaration.
And yes—it is that.

But biblically, it is more than a declaration.
It is a burial.

Paul does not say we were merely inspired by Christ.
He says we were **buried with Him**.

That means baptism marks the end of an old life pattern:

- the old loyalties
- the old identity
- the old reactions
- the old agreements with sin
- the old self-built way of living

This is why baptism is such a serious line in the sand.

It is not merely the start of "being religious."
It is the crossing point where one life is being left behind
and another life is meant to begin.

**Baptism is not just the celebration of a decision.
It is the funeral of an old direction.**

And funerals are meant to mean something.

2. What Goes Under the Water Is Meant to Lose Its Rule

Jesus gave us the pattern in the Jordan.

Not because He needed cleansing from sin—but because He revealed the path of surrender, obedience, and Spirit-filled emergence.

Romans 6 now tells us what that pattern means for us.

The old man—the self shaped by sin, fear, appetite, pride, survival, and separation—is not meant to remain in charge.

That does not mean temptation instantly disappears.
It does not mean the soul is suddenly fully healed.
It does not mean the body stops having cravings.

But it does mean something real has changed.

The old ruler has been challenged.
The old agreement has been broken.
The old identity has been confronted by a greater one.

In Christ, you are not being invited to improve the old man.
You are being invited to stop letting him lead.

**Baptism is not the old you getting cleaned up.
It is the old you losing the right to drive.**

That is why baptism matters.

It is not merely saying, *"I believe in Jesus."*
It is saying:

"The old me is no longer authorized to lead this life."

3. Washed, Renewed, and Meant to Come Up Different

Scripture also speaks of washing and renewal.

Titus 3:5 (KJV)
Not by works of righteousness which we have done, but according to his mercy he saved us, by the washing of regeneration, and renewing of the Holy Ghost;

Notice how beautifully this aligns with everything we have been building:

- not by works
- not by ritual performance
- not by human effort
- but by mercy
- by washing
- by regeneration
- by renewing
- by the Holy Ghost

This is not mere water language.
This is transformation language.

Water baptism points visibly to an invisible reality:

- cleansing from the old
- separation from the former life
- entrance into a new identity
- and the beginning of a new walk

This is why baptism should never be reduced to tradition.

It is the visible doorway of a deeper spiritual truth.

The water is the sign.
The death is the shift.
The Spirit is the life.

And if the doctrine is not taught clearly, many people come out of the water with wet skin—but unchanged patterns.

That is not because the symbol failed.
It is because the new life was never clearly shown.

4. Baptism Is Not Just What You Entered—It Is What You Emerged Into

By now, the chapter is locking together.

In Section 1, we saw that baptism is not meant to be reduced to denominational confusion or religious ceremony.
In Section 2, we saw Jesus enter the waters and emerge under the Father's voice and the Spirit's presence.
In Section 3, we asked the deeper question:

What are you actually being immersed into?

Now here in Section 4, the answer becomes clearer.

You are not only being immersed into water.
You are being immersed into **death to the old life** and **newness of life in Christ**.

Not 20 percent.
Not 75 percent.
Not "a better version of your old self."

Buried with Christ.
Raised with Christ.
Washed.

Renewed.
Repositioned.

If baptism marks the line in the sand, then what you rise
into must be more than vague Christian language.

You rise into the revealed nature of God.

You rise into mercy.
You rise into compassion.
You rise into patience.
You rise into loving-kindness.
You rise into truth.
You rise into forgiveness.
You rise into justice.

Not just as ideas.
As the atmosphere of the new life.

Baptism is not only leaving the old shore.
It is entering the flow of God's own heart.

5. The Holy Ghost, Fire, and the Life That Follows

John baptized with water, but he made it clear that water
was not the final word.

Matthew 3:11 (KJV)
I indeed baptize you with water unto repentance:
but he that cometh after me is mightier than I... he
shall baptize you with the Holy Ghost, and with
fire:

Water baptism points forward.
It is not the end of the journey.
It is the beginning of a life that must now be filled, refined,
and empowered.

Jesus stepped into the water in obedience—
and the Spirit descended.

The disciples came into alignment and obedience—
and in one accord, the Spirit came with power.

There is a pattern here.

Not a mechanical formula.
But a revealed pattern:

- surrender
- obedience
- alignment
- emergence
- empowerment

This is why baptism should never be taught as a finish line.

It is a threshold.
A doorway.
A line in the sand.

And on the other side is not merely church attendance.

On the other side is a life meant to be:

- led by the Spirit
- refined by fire
- washed in truth
- transformed in love
- and increasingly formed **In Christ**

Water may mark the moment.
But the Holy Ghost marks the life.

Closing Reinforcement

So no—baptism is not merely about what you went into.

It is about what was meant to end there.
And it is about what was meant to rise.

If the old life is still pulling the strings...
if the old fears still dominate...
if the old appetites still keep dragging you back toward the
same shoreline...
then the next question is not whether baptism mattered.

The next question is whether the deeper work has been
understood...
and whether the old man is still being allowed to call you
home.

Because many people come out of the water—
but part of them is still standing on the shore.

Some bodies leave the water.
But some old agreements never do.

And that is exactly where we must go next.

Baptism draws a line.
But many believers still feel the pull of the old life after they
cross it.

Why?

Why do some step into the waters
and still drift back toward the same fears,
the same habits,
the same old reactions,
and the same old identity?

What keeps pulling a person back to shore
when God has already called them into deeper
waters?

That is where we turn next.
Because sometimes the problem is not that you were never
baptized.

It is that the old life was never fully released,
the soul was never retrained,
and the deeper work of surrender was never fully embraced.

**The water may have been crossed.
But the heart kept building a dock.**

SECTION 5 —
WHAT KEEPS PEOPLE FROM
LIVING WHAT BAPTISM MEANS?

Why the crossing must become a life,
not just a moment

Anchor Scripture:
Luke 9:62 (KJV) — *"And Jesus said unto him, No man, having put his hand to the plough, and looking back, is fit for the kingdom of God."*

Baptism is often treated as a moment of celebration.
A public declaration.
A church milestone.
A memory.

And in one sense, it is all of those things.

But biblically, baptism is not merely the moment you stepped into the water.
It is the line in the sand where one life ends and another begins.

That is why so many people have been baptized...
and yet still live as though nothing really changed.

Because the ceremony happened...
but the crossing did not.

It is possible to go into the water sincerely...
and still come back out with no real understanding of what you just agreed to.

Not because your heart was false.
Not because God was absent.
But because no one clearly told you what baptism was meant to mean.

Many were told to believe.
Told to confess.
Told to get baptized.

But they were never clearly taught that baptism was meant to become a pattern of life **In Christ**—
a life immersed in the anointed presence of **God's love** like Jesus.

And when the pattern is not taught,
the old pattern quietly returns.

1. The Problem Is Not the Water — It Is the Return Path

Most people do not struggle because baptism was meaningless.

They struggle because the old life was still waiting for them
when they got out.

The same reactions.
The same fears.
The same habits.
The same emotional loops.
The same survival patterns.

The water marked a moment.
But the mind was not renewed.
The heart was not retrained.
The direction was not reinforced.
And the new life was not clearly defined.

So when pressure came,
they went back to what was familiar.

This is why the enemy fights clarity.

If he cannot stop the baptism,
he will try to empty it of meaning.

If he cannot keep a person out of the water,
he will try to make sure they come back out unchanged.

Because confusion is one of the easiest bridges back to the
old man.

And if the old man still feels like home,
the new life will feel unnatural until it is practiced.

That is why baptism must be taught as more than an event.
It must be taught as a crossing into a new way of being.

Not just **for Christ**.
But **In Christ**.

**Baptism is not just where you went down.
It is the line that tells the old life it no longer owns
you.**

2. Marriage Helps Us Understand the Weight of the Crossing

Marriage gives us a recognized human picture.

A wedding is not just a party.
Not just a dress, a ring, a kiss, and some photos.

It is a covenant crossing.

Two people stand before witnesses and say, in effect:

**The old way is over.
A new life begins here.**

That does not mean temptation disappears.
That does not mean selfishness disappears.
That does not mean conflict disappears.

It means the line has been drawn.

And from that moment on, the relationship is no longer
meant to be approached like it was before.

That is why this line matters so much:

**Many marriages fail because the line in the sand
was too easy to jump back over.**

That is not just a statement about marriage.
It is a statement about covenant.

If the old exits remain emotionally available...
if retreat is always mentally prepared...
if self-preservation remains the highest instinct...

then pressure will eventually expose what was never truly surrendered.

The same is true with baptism.

If baptism is treated as inspiration instead of covenant...
if the old life is still being quietly preserved...
if Egypt is still being romanticized in the imagination...
then the crossing becomes symbolic only.

But biblical baptism is not meant to be symbolic only.

It is meant to say:

I am not who I was.
I do not belong to that life anymore.
I have crossed into another pattern.

That does not mean you never struggle.
It means struggle no longer defines your identity.

It means when you stumble,
you do not run back across the line.

You rise again **In Christ**.

3. The Real Battle Is What You Keep Agreeing With After the Water

Many people think the biggest battle after baptism is sin.

But often the deeper battle is agreement.

What story are you still agreeing with?

What identity are you still agreeing with?

What emotional pattern are you still calling "just who I am"?

What inherited reaction are you still excusing because it feels familiar?

Because baptism says something radical:

The old man is not your master anymore.

That does not mean the flesh stops talking.
It means it no longer has the right to lead.

That does not mean the soul stops reacting.
It means the soul must now be retrained under truth.

That does not mean temptation vanishes.
It means temptation is no longer your identity.

This is where many believers become discouraged.

They expected baptism to remove the struggle.
But baptism was never meant to remove the need for growth.

It was meant to establish the new direction of growth.

It was the line.
The burial.
The public crossing.
The yes.

But the yes must now be walked out.

This is why scripture calls believers to:

- put off the old man
- put on the new man
- renew the mind
- walk in the Spirit
- abide in Christ
- reckon yourselves dead indeed unto sin, but alive unto God

Because baptism begins a pattern.
It does not replace discipleship.

**Baptism announces the crossing.
Discipleship teaches you how to live on the other
side of it.**

4. What Keeps the Line Strong?

So what actually keeps a person from drifting back?

Not fear.
Not religious pressure.
Not trying harder.

Love.

Not sentimental love.
Not emotional hype.
But the living pattern of **God's love** revealed in Christ.

People do not stay dead to the old life
by staring at death.

They stay faithful to the new life
by discovering that what they crossed into is better.

This is true in marriage too.

The strongest marriages are not preserved merely by rules.

They are preserved because the covenant becomes
inhabited.

Shared life.
Shared sacrifice.
Shared mercy.
Shared patience.
Shared truth.

Shared forgiveness.
Shared love.

In other words, the covenant becomes lived.

That is exactly what baptism was always pointing toward.

Not merely a break from the old life—
but immersion into a new one.

And what is that new one?

To live **In Christ**
is to flow in the anointed presence of **God's love** like Jesus.

That is not just a doctrine.
That is the life after the water.

That is what keeps the line from becoming just a memory.

Because once a person begins to taste the mercy,
compassion, patience, loving-kindness, truth, forgiveness,
and justice of God as a lived reality...
the old life may still call,
but it no longer looks like home.

5. The Question Is Not "Were You Baptized?" — But "What Did You Cross Into?"

This is where the chapter becomes deeply personal.

Not to condemn you.
Not to make you question every sincere step you have ever
taken.

But to ask the right question.

Not:

Did you get wet?

Not:

Did people clap?

Not:

Did you have the ceremony?

But:

What did you believe that crossing meant?

What old identity are you still treating like it has authority?

What line in the sand keeps becoming easy for you to step back over?

Have you truly begun to live the life your baptism was pointing toward?

Because if not, this chapter is not here to shame you.

It is here to call you forward.

The good news is not that you must be perfect after the water.

The good news is that **God's love** has made a way for you to keep walking forward **In Christ**, even when your soul is still learning the path.

The old life may still echo.
The flesh may still protest.
The soul may still wobble.

But the line is still there.

And if you have crossed in faith,
you do not need to go back to start again.

You need to understand what you crossed into...
and keep walking.

Because baptism was never meant to be the end of a church moment.

It was meant to be the beginning of a life.

A life where the old man is no longer your home.
A life where the soul is being retrained by truth.
A life where the Spirit leads.
A life where covenant is not merely declared, but inhabited.
A life where what went into the water is no longer meant to rule what came out.

**Baptism is not the finish line of conversion.
It is the crossing line into life In Christ.**

And once that line is understood,
the next question becomes unavoidable:

**If baptism marks the crossing...
what does mature spiritual growth look like after the crossing?**

Because the journey does not end in the water.

It continues into discernment, stability, and spiritual maturity.

And that is where we now turn next.

Closing Anchor

**Many people have crossed the line in public...
but have never been taught how to live on the other
side of it.**

**Baptism is not merely the line in the sand.
It is the beginning of learning how to stay there —
In Christ.**

CHAPTER 4 — LAYING ON OF HANDS

The shift from isolated belief into impartation, blessing, healing, commissioning, and the shared life of the Body

Hebrews 6:1–2 (KJV)
"Therefore leaving the principles of the doctrine of Christ, let us go on unto perfection... of the doctrine of baptisms, and of laying on of hands..."

Secondary Anchor Scripture — 2 Timothy 1:6 (KJV)
"Wherefore I put thee in remembrance that thou stir up the gift of God, which is in thee by the putting on of my hands."

Laying on of hands is one of the most misunderstood foundations in the doctrine of Christ because many people have seen it practiced without ever being taught what it means.

For some, it has been reduced to a church custom. For others, it has become a strange or overhyped moment surrounded by emotion, pressure, or confusion.

But in scripture, laying on of hands is not presented as a theatrical act, nor as a religious extra.

It is one of the six foundation stones of spiritual maturity. That alone should tell us something important: this matters more than many people realize.

At its simplest level, laying on of hands is the visible expression of spiritual agreement, blessing, support, transfer, recognition, and participation.

It is not magic. It is not manipulation. And it is not a shortcut around relationship with God. It is a God-given pattern that reveals something deeper about how life **In Christ** was always meant to function.

We were never designed to walk alone. The kingdom of God is deeply relational, and the laying on of hands is one of the clearest pictures in scripture that grace, healing, encouragement, commissioning, and even spiritual strengthening often flow through connection.

This is where Chapter 4 becomes deeply important in the journey of **The Doctrine of Christ**.

Repentance turned us away from dead works.

Faith toward God taught us where true support comes from.

The doctrine of baptisms showed us the line in the sand where one life ends and another begins.

Now this next foundation reveals that life **In Christ** is not merely personal—it is also participational. God's love does not only restore the individual; it joins the individual into a living Body. Hands in scripture often become the symbol of that reality: blessing fathers to sons, healing flowing to the sick, leaders commissioning workers, apostles affirming grace, and believers strengthening one another in the presence of God.

This chapter will help us recover the simplicity and power of this foundation. Not every hand laid on a person is automatically holy, and not every spiritual moment is genuine simply because it feels intense.

Scripture gives us both beauty and caution. But it also shows us something essential: when rightly understood, laying on of hands is one of the practical ways the life of God is shared among His people. It is one of the places where heaven touches earth through surrendered human vessels. In that sense, it is not merely about hands at all. It is about connection, alignment, transmission, and the relational flow of God's love **In Christ**.

If baptism marked the crossing point, laying on of hands begins to show us what happens after the crossing. You are not only called out of the old life—you are received into a living pattern. You are blessed, strengthened, prayed over, healed, affirmed, and sometimes sent.

This chapter is about that shift: from private faith into shared participation; from merely believing alone into becoming part of the living movement of the Body of Christ.

Chapter Flow — The Five Section Journey

1. The Hands That Carry the Blessing

This first section introduces the doctrine clearly and relationally. It dismantles confusion by showing that laying on of hands is not religious theatre but a biblical pattern of blessing, agreement, and support.

It helps the reader recognize that God often uses human connection as part of how His love is expressed.

2. Jesus Touched What Others Avoided

This section reveals the doctrine through the life of Jesus. His hands were not casual—they carried compassion, healing, restoration, and power.

Here we anchor the chapter in the pattern of Christ, where touch becomes a visible expression of God's love reaching the broken, the sick, and the outcast.

3. What Are You Actually Receiving?

This section brings the doctrine into personal recognition. Not every influence is healthy, and not every spiritual transfer is from God.

Here we help the reader discern what kind of agreement, atmosphere, identity, and direction they have been opening themselves to—both naturally and spiritually.

4. Stir Up the Gift Within You

This section reinforces the doctrine through the language of impartation, activation, remembrance, and shared grace.

It explores how scripture presents laying on of hands not only in healing, but in encouragement, strengthening, commissioning, and awakening what God has already placed within a person.

5. Who Has the Right to Speak Into Your Life?

This final section evaluates the reader's posture toward spiritual influence, community, and accountability.

It brings the chapter to a mature and practical close by asking who we allow near enough to shape us, pray for us, affirm us, and send us—and bridges naturally into the next foundation stone.

SECTION 1 — THE HANDS THAT CARRY THE BLESSING

God often moves His love through people before He moves them into purpose.

Core Scriptures:
Hebrews 6:1–2 (KJV)
"Therefore leaving the principles of the doctrine of Christ, let us go on unto perfection... of the doctrine of baptisms, and of laying on of hands..."

Acts 16:1–2 (KJV)
"Then came he to Derbe and Lystra: and, behold, a certain disciple was there, named Timotheus... Which was well reported of by the brethren that were at Lystra and Iconium."

For many people, the phrase *laying on of hands* immediately creates tension.
Some picture emotional religious meetings.
Others picture manipulation, performance, or spiritual theatre.
Some have seen it done badly.
Some have seen it done without understanding.
And many have never been taught what it actually means at all.

But Hebrews does not place the laying on of hands among the strange outer edges of the faith.
It places it among the **foundations**.
That alone should make us pause.
If this doctrine is part of the foundation, then it is not meant

to be feared, mocked, or ignored.
It is meant to be understood.

At its simplest, the laying on of hands is not magic.

It is not superstition.
It is not the transfer of human power.
It is a **biblical pattern of blessing, agreement, support, recognition, commissioning, healing, and connection**through which God often makes His love tangible.
It is one of the ways the invisible becomes visible.
It is one of the ways support becomes felt.

Most people have already experienced the principle of this doctrine long before they ever had language for it.

You may not have called it *laying on of hands*, but you have probably felt what it means.

A father placing a hand on a child's shoulder before a hard conversation.
A mother holding a hurting son or daughter when words are not enough.
A friend embracing you in grief when your soul has run out of sentences.
Someone praying for you with one hand on your back while your world is shaking.
A quiet moment where support became physical, and somehow the room changed.

That is why this doctrine matters more than many realize.
Spiritual life was never designed to be lived in isolation.
Before a person is sent, strengthened, healed, or commissioned, they are often first **seen**.
Before the next step becomes clear, someone trustworthy often comes close enough to encourage, affirm, or strengthen what God is already doing.

The Father has always had a habit of using people as part of His pattern.

That is why Timothy is such a powerful chapter witness. Before he becomes a pastor, a son in the faith, or a man entrusted with real responsibility, he is first a young disciple who is **known**, **spoken well of**, and **drawn near**.

Before hands are laid on him in any formal sense, he is already standing in a living pattern of spiritual support. And that is where this doctrine begins—not with spectacle, but with love made tangible.

1. The doctrine is often misunderstood because people remember the form, but not the purpose.

When people hear the words *laying on of hands*, they often think of the outward act first.
A hand on a shoulder.
A hand on a head.
A prayer line.
A dramatic moment.
A public setting.

But scripture is not primarily trying to make us stare at the **gesture**.
Scripture is teaching us to understand the **meaning**.

The act itself is simple.
Human.
Ordinary, even.

What gives it weight is not the skin.
It is the **context**.

In the same way that baptism is not just about getting wet,
the laying on of hands is not just about being touched.
It is about what that touch is **saying**, what it is **agreeing
with**, and what it is **representing** in the sight of God.

Throughout scripture, hands can signify blessing.
They can signify identification.
They can signify agreement.
They can signify impartation.
They can signify healing.
They can signify being set apart for a task.
They can signify support.
They can signify that heaven is not treating this person as
invisible.

That last one matters.

Because many people can survive hardship better than they
can survive feeling unseen.

And one of the quiet beauties of this doctrine is that it
reminds us: **God's love often comes close before it
sends us forward.**

To live **In Christ** is not to become more isolated, more
suspicious, or more detached from the Body.
It is to begin recognizing that the anointed presence of
God's love often flows through real people, in real
moments, in ways that strengthen the journey.

So before we ask what laying on of hands *does*, we must first
understand what it *is*.

It is not religious theatre.
It is not spiritual superstition.
It is not emotional manipulation.

It is a relational doctrine.
A doctrine of support.

A doctrine of nearness.
A doctrine of blessing.

A doctrine that says the Father often chooses to let His love
be **felt** through the Body of Christ.

2. Before Timothy was commissioned, he was already being carried by a pattern of support.

The first thing scripture tells us about Timothy is not that he
preached to crowds.
Not that he worked miracles.
Not that he held office.
Not even that Paul laid hands on him.

The first thing we are told is that he was there.

A certain disciple.

A young man already in the environment of faith.
Already growing.
Already known.
Already carrying a good report.

"Which was well reported of by the brethren..."

That is a beautiful line.

Before Timothy becomes a leader, he is first a young
believer who has already been **seen by the community**.
Others have noticed something in him.
Others can testify to his character.
Others can speak life over his path.
There is already evidence that the grace of God is forming
something in him.

That is not a side note.
That is part of the doctrine.

Because the laying on of hands does not begin with a ceremony.
It begins with a pattern.

A pattern where the Father uses trusted relationships.
A pattern where spiritual life grows in the presence of witness.
A pattern where what God is doing in secret is often recognized by others before it is publicly released.

Timothy did not become Timothy in a vacuum.

He was nurtured by the faith of his mother and grandmother.
He was noticed by the brethren.
He was drawn near by Paul.
He was strengthened by instruction.
He was entrusted over time.

Then later, hands were laid on him in ways that marked, confirmed, and strengthened what God was already doing.

That order matters.

Because in our time, many people want the public moment without the hidden formation.
They want the microphone without the witness.
They want the commissioning without the character.
They want the spiritual badge without the relational process.

But Timothy's life shows us something healthier.

God's love often builds a person through **support before spotlight**.

The laying on of hands is not the invention of calling.
It is often the recognition, blessing, strengthening, or
confirming of something the Father has already been
shaping.

That makes the doctrine safer.
And deeper.
And far more beautiful.

Because it means this is not about chasing moments.
It is about learning how the Father builds people **In Christ**.

3. The hands around your life have already been shaping you.

Whether we acknowledge it or not, every person is shaped
by the hands that have touched their life.

Some hands carried blessing.
Some hands carried pressure.
Some hands carried correction.
Some hands carried violence.
Some hands carried comfort.
Some hands carried neglect.
Some hands pushed us forward.
Some hands held us back.

That is why this doctrine is so personal.

Because it is not merely about what happens in a church
meeting.
It is about the reality that human beings are deeply affected
by **support, agreement, affirmation, and contact**.
We are not floating minds.
We are embodied people.
Body, soul, and spirit all register what comes near.

A father placing a hand on a son's shoulder can say, *I believe in you.*
A mother holding a child in grief can say, *You are not alone.*
A friend praying with one hand on another friend can say, *We are standing together.*
A mature believer blessing someone can say, *What God is doing in you matters.*

In the wrong hands, touch can wound.
But in the right hands, under the truth of God's love, touch can reassure, steady, strengthen, and bless.

This is why the doctrine must be understood in the light of **God's love**, not in the shadow of religious abuse.

Because where the world has twisted touch into control, Christ restores it into **support**.
Where manipulation has made people suspicious, the Father still intends His Body to become a place of safe blessing.
Where some have used outward acts to draw attention to themselves, Jesus always pointed beyond the act to the Father.

And if we miss that, we will either reject the doctrine entirely or imitate it poorly.

But if we understand it rightly, we begin to see something precious:

Sometimes the laying on of hands is not primarily about power.
Sometimes it is about **presence**.

Sometimes the first miracle is simply that someone is no longer carrying the burden alone.

4. Jesus Himself shows us that heaven is not afraid to come close.

When we look at Jesus, we do not find a distant Savior avoiding human contact.
We find the opposite.

He touched lepers.
He touched the sick.
He touched blind eyes.
He took Jairus' daughter by the hand.
He laid His hands on little children and blessed them.

Mark 10:16 (KJV)
"And he took them up in his arms, put his hands upon them, and blessed them."

That verse alone dismantles much of the confusion.

Jesus was not performing a religious stunt.
He was revealing the nature of the Kingdom.

The holy did not withdraw from the needy.
The clean did not recoil from the unclean.
The love of God came near.

That is the pattern.

The laying on of hands is not an odd religious extra tacked onto Christianity.
It belongs to the larger pattern of **incarnational love**—the reality that God's love in Christ comes near, touches what is broken, blesses what is vulnerable, and strengthens what is being formed.

This is why the doctrine must always stay connected to Jesus.

If it becomes disconnected from Him, it can become theatrical.
If it stays rooted in Him, it becomes beautiful.

In Christ, the laying on of hands is not about drawing attention to the hand.
It is about revealing the heart behind it.

The hand is not the source.
The Father is.

The hand is simply the point of contact.
The love is His.
The healing is His.
The strengthening is His.
The blessing is His.

And that is why this doctrine belongs among the foundations.

Because the Kingdom is not merely declared.

It is often **expressed**.

5. Before we talk about impartation, we must first ask whether we understand safe blessing.

Before we explore commissioning, healing, ordination, impartation, or the later moments in Timothy's life, it is worth asking something simpler:

Do we even understand the holiness of **safe blessing**?

Do we understand what it means to come near another person in a way that reflects the Father's heart?

Do we understand what it means to support without controlling?
To affirm without flattering?
To pray without performing?
To bless without needing attention?
To strengthen without trying to own the outcome?

Those questions matter because the laying on of hands is not powerful simply because it is dramatic.

It is powerful when it is **true**.

True to scripture.
True to Christ.
True to love.
True to the heart of the Father.

And this is where many readers may need to gently locate themselves.

- When you think of spiritual touch, do you feel peace —or tension?
- Have you seen this doctrine expressed in a way that reflects **God's love**, or in a way that made you wary?
- Have you ever been strengthened simply because someone came close, prayed sincerely, and reminded you that you were not alone?

Those are not trick questions.
They are doorway questions.

Because before the doctrine becomes something you understand in theology, it often has to become something you recognize in life.

And if you have never known safe blessing, then this chapter may begin by healing your understanding before it ever expands your vocabulary.

That is a worthy beginning.

Because the laying on of hands is not first about spiritual force.

It is first about whether the life of **God's love In Christ** has become tangible enough to be felt through His people.

Closing Anchor

Before Timothy ever became a man publicly entrusted with responsibility, he was first a young man surrounded by faith, known by others, and drawn into the care of someone older and wiser.

That is how the Father often works.

He does not usually begin with the platform.
He begins with the pattern.
He begins with witness.
He begins with relationship.
He begins with hands that carry blessing.

And in Timothy's story, those hands will soon do more than comfort.

They will begin to **recognize the call**.

SECTION 2 — THE HANDS THAT RECOGNIZE THE CALL

How Timothy moves from quiet faithfulness into public confirmation

Core Scripture:
Neglect not the gift that is in thee, which was given thee by prophecy, with the laying on of the hands of the presbytery.
— **1 Timothy 4:14 (KJV)**

There are moments in life when a person has something real in them long before anyone around them has words for it.

A quiet strength.
A faithful spirit.
A willingness to serve.
A steadiness under pressure.
A tenderness toward God.
A fire that has not yet found its language.

That is often how calling begins.

Not with a stage.
Not with a title.
Not with a microphone.
But with hidden faithfulness.

Before a man is publicly recognized, he is usually privately becoming.

And that is why the doctrine of laying on of hands matters so deeply.

Because in Scripture, laying on of hands is not merely about *imparting* something new.
Often, it is also about *recognizing* what God has already been growing in secret.

The hand does not always create the call.
Sometimes the hand confirms it.

That is where Timothy becomes one of the clearest witnesses in the New Testament.

He did not burst onto the pages of Scripture as a celebrity preacher.
He appears as a young man already carrying a good reputation, already marked by sincere faith, already being formed by the unseen work of God.

And then, at the right moment, faithful hands came upon that hidden life and said, in effect:

We see it too.

That is a holy thing.

Because many people live with real grace on their life but have never been recognized clearly enough to step forward with confidence.

They carry love.
They carry wisdom.
They carry steadiness.
They carry compassion.
They carry gifts that could strengthen others.

But without confirmation, many stay hesitant.
Without support, many stay small.
Without trusted voices, many keep second-guessing what God may already be doing.

This is why laying on of hands is not religious theatre.

It is one of the ways the Body of Christ says:

We see the grace of God on your life.
We stand with what God is doing.
And we bless you to move forward.

That is not a small thing.

A man can spend years wondering if he is imagining the call.
One clear moment of godly recognition can help him stop
circling and start walking.

Timothy's story helps us see this beautifully.

He was not the loudest man in the room.
He was not introduced to us as naturally dominant, forceful,
or untouchable.

In many ways, Timothy feels more relatable than that.

Young.
Developing.
Trusted, but still growing.
Sincere, but needing strengthening.
Faithful, but needing courage.

That makes him a perfect witness for this chapter.

Because the doctrine of laying on of hands is not only for
spiritual giants.

It is for real people.

It is for sons and daughters in the faith.
It is for those being raised, strengthened, commissioned,
and encouraged.
It is for those moving from hidden formation into visible
responsibility.

And that movement matters.

Because there is a difference between *having potential* and
being sent.
There is a difference between *private growth* and *public
confirmation*.
There is a difference between *hoping you are called* and
*being recognized by those who already carry weight in the
Spirit*.

Timothy steps into that line.

Not by striving.
Not by self-promotion.
Not by building a name.

But by faithfulness, character, and the witness of others.

1. Timothy Was Already Becoming Before He Was Publicly Recognized

When Timothy first enters the biblical story, he is not introduced as a blank slate.

Scripture says:

Then came he to Derbe and Lystra: and, behold, a certain disciple was there, named Timotheus... which was well reported of by the brethren that were at Lystra and Iconium. — Acts 16:1–2 (KJV)

That is a powerful beginning.

Before Paul lays hands on Timothy...
before Timothy is strengthened into ministry...
before letters are written to him...
before his name becomes part of the New Testament record...

He is already *well reported of.*

That means something had already been seen.

People around him had already noticed his life.
They had already seen sincerity.
They had already seen reliability.
They had already seen enough to speak well of him.

This matters because the doctrine of laying on of hands is not meant to replace character.

It is not a shortcut around formation.
It is not a spiritual badge for the ambitious.
It is not a fast-track for the self-promoting.

In the biblical pattern, the hands often come *after* the hidden work has already begun.

First the root.
Then the fruit.
Then the recognition.

That is a safer order.

Because when recognition comes before formation, people can collapse under the weight of what they were not yet ready to carry.

But when God forms a person in hidden places first, public confirmation becomes a strengthening instead of a burden.

Timothy appears in exactly that kind of order. He was already becoming before he was ever publicly affirmed.

And many readers need to hear that.

You may already be carrying more of God's work in your life than you realize.

You may think you are "not there yet," because no one has formally said anything over you.

But heaven is not confused by silence.

God can be building deeply in a person long before others know how to name it.

A steady prayer life no one sees.
A heart that naturally moves toward mercy.
A burden for people.
A quiet hunger for truth.
A willingness to serve without applause.
A growing distaste for empty religion and a deeper desire for what is real In Christ.

Those things matter.

That is often where calling begins.

Not in spotlight moments.
In hidden alignment.

Timothy was not invented by the laying on of hands. He was recognized through it. And that distinction protects this doctrine from becoming mystical in the wrong way.

The hand matters.
The prayer matters.
The prophetic witness matters.
The public confirmation matters.

But the hand is not meant to cover emptiness. It is meant to acknowledge life.

That is a word the modern church needs badly.

Because too often people are platformed before they are proven.
Promoted before they are formed.
Celebrated before they are steady.

Then when pressure comes, everything shakes.

But Timothy gives us another pattern.

Faithfulness first.
Reputation second.

Recognition third.
Responsibility after that.

That is wisdom.

That is love.

And that is part of how God protects both the person and the people they will later serve.

2. Paul Did Not Just See Ability — He Saw a Son Worth Strengthening

When Paul encountered Timothy, he did not simply find a useful helper.

He found someone worth investing in.

That distinction matters.

The kingdom of God is not built merely by spotting talent. It is built by recognizing grace, nurturing maturity, and strengthening people in God's love.

Paul saw something in Timothy that went deeper than skill.

He saw sincerity.
He saw teachability.
He saw a man who could carry truth.
He saw someone whose life could be entrusted with weight over time.

Later, Paul writes:

*When I call to remembrance the unfeigned faith that is in thee, which dwelt first in thy grandmother Lois, and thy mother Eunice... — **2 Timothy 1:5 (KJV)***

That is beautiful.

Timothy's story is not presented as raw ambition.
It is presented as inherited sincerity, nurtured faith, and
faithful formation.

His faith was not fake.
It was not performative.
It was not loud for the sake of being seen.

It was *unfeigned*.

Real.

That is exactly the kind of life laying on of hands should
surround.

Because laying on of hands, in its healthiest form, is not
about creating spiritual celebrities.

It is about strengthening real people to carry real
responsibility in God's love.

Paul did not appear to Timothy as a talent scout.

He appeared as a spiritual father.

He saw the seed...
and he helped protect the growth.

That matters because one of the deepest functions of laying
on of hands is relational, not merely ceremonial.

It says:

You are not stepping into this alone.

That may be one of the most powerful things a person can
hear.

Because many people can survive uncertainty if they know
someone godly is walking with them.

The call itself can feel overwhelming.
The responsibility can feel heavy.
The future can feel unclear.

But support changes the atmosphere.

A father placing a hand on a shoulder.
A mother praying over a child.
An elder blessing a younger believer.
A trusted leader recognizing grace and saying, "Keep going."

This is not just symbolism.

This is how confidence is often built in the kingdom.

Not through ego.
Through support.

Not through hype.
Through witness.

Not through self-assertion.
Through love.

Timothy becomes such a strong witness here because his life
shows us that public ministry often grows best out of private
relationship.

Paul did not merely use him.
He formed him.

He wrote to him.
He warned him.
He encouraged him.
He reminded him.
He strengthened him when fear, youth, weakness, and
pressure could have made him shrink back.

That is the environment where laying on of hands makes
sense.

Because the hands are not magic hands.

They are covenantal hands.

They are relational hands.

They are hands that say:

**We are not just noticing your gift.
We are taking responsibility to help you carry it
well.**

That is weighty.

And if the church recovered *that* understanding, this
doctrine would become beautiful again.

Not weird.
Not theatrical.
Not forced.

Beautiful.

Because many people do not need more noise.

They need one godly person who can see what God is doing
and stand beside it.

That is what Paul became for Timothy.

And that is what the doctrine begins to reveal.

3. The Laying On of Hands Brought Hidden Grace Into Public Clarity

At some point in Timothy's journey, what had been growing
quietly became publicly confirmed.

That is where the doctrine steps fully into view.

Paul later writes:

Neglect not the gift that is in thee, which was given thee by prophecy, with the laying on of the hands of the presbytery. — 1 Timothy 4:14 (KJV)

And again:

Wherefore I put thee in remembrance that thou stir up the gift of God, which is in thee by the putting on of my hands. — 2 Timothy 1:6 (KJV)

Now we are standing in the formal passages.

And notice how rich they are.

There is **gift**.
There is **prophecy**.
There is **laying on of hands**.
There is **presbytery** — a recognized body of elders.
There is **Paul's own hands** in personal fatherly confirmation.

This is not casual.

This is not random.

This is a public moment of spiritual recognition and strengthening.

The hidden life had reached a point where the Body of Christ could say, with weight and order:

This grace is real.
This direction is right.
This man is to be strengthened for what is ahead.

That is exactly what this doctrine protects.

It protects the transition from private becoming to public responsibility.

It creates a moment where calling is not left vague.

A gift may already be present.
A burden may already be present.
A grace may already be present.

But when the church recognizes it properly, prays over it, and lays hands in agreement, something becomes clearer.

Not necessarily because God suddenly started the work that day…
but because the work was now being *named, affirmed, and strengthened* in order.

That order matters.

Especially in a generation that often confuses desire with calling.

Wanting something is not the same as being sent.
Feeling stirred is not always the same as being ready.
Being passionate is not always the same as being proven.

Timothy's story gives us a safer path.

A life is observed.
A faith is witnessed.
A character is tested.
A grace is recognized.
A word is spoken.
Hands are laid.
The person is strengthened.

That is beautiful order.

And it is not just for "ministry jobs."

This pattern reaches wider than pulpits.

A mother may be strengthened to carry her home.
A father may be strengthened to lead with patience instead
of fear.
A young believer may be strengthened to serve.
A wounded saint may be strengthened to begin again.
A missionary may be sent.
A teacher may be recognized.
A helper may be blessed.
An elder may be confirmed.
A person called to hidden faithfulness may be strengthened
just as surely as someone called to public preaching.

Because the doctrine is bigger than platform.

It is about support, recognition, agreement, and
strengthening in the will of God.

Timothy shows us this clearly.

And once you see it, the doctrine starts to come alive.

Not as ritual.
As relational order.

Not as superstition.
As embodied agreement.

Not as spiritual performance.
As the Body of Christ helping a person step into what God is
already doing.

4. Many People Stay Small Because No One Ever Helped Name What God Was Doing

This is where Timothy's story moves from biblical history into the reader's own life.

Because there are many people who have lived with genuine grace on their life... and yet remain hesitant, unsure, or half-hidden.

Not because God has failed them.
Not because the call is unreal.
But because no one ever clearly helped them recognize what was happening.

That creates drift.

A person feels drawn toward something but doubts themselves.
They care deeply but do not know if it is valid.
They sense a burden but assume it is just emotion.
They have unusual compassion, insight, steadiness, or hunger for truth, but because no trusted voice has ever affirmed it, they keep shrinking back.

This is more common than people realize.

Some are carrying a shepherd's heart and think they are just "too emotional."
Some are carrying wisdom and think they are just "older and tired."
Some are carrying intercession and think they are just "burdened all the time."
Some are carrying discernment and think they are just "hard to please."
Some are carrying a teaching grace and think they are just "always explaining things."

Sometimes what you have been trying to suppress is the very thing heaven has been trying to grow.

That does not mean every inner urge is a calling.
Timothy protects us from that mistake.

The call must be weighed.
Character must matter.
Fruit must matter.
Witness must matter.
Order must matter.

But it also means this:

God often places something in a person before that person fully understands it.

And one of the blessings of healthy laying on of hands is that it can bring holy clarity where there has only been uncertainty.

A trusted voice says:

"I see this in you."
"This is real."
"Keep walking."
"Do not neglect what God has placed in you."
"Stir it up."
"We are with you."

Those words can change the trajectory of a life.

Not because they replace God's voice.
Because they *confirm* it.

That is why this doctrine should feel deeply human.

Timothy was not merely given a ministry procedure.

He was strengthened in a relationship.
He was recognized in community.
He was confirmed in order.
He was reminded not to neglect what had been placed in him.

That sounds a lot like many of us.

Because most people do not need someone to flatter them.

They need someone to recognize the grace of God honestly.

Not exaggerate it.
Not manipulate it.
Not manufacture it.

Just see it.

And when that happens in God's love, something powerful occurs.

Fear loosens.
Confusion clears.
Direction sharpens.
Responsibility becomes weighty but possible.

The soul stops spinning quite so hard.

Because now the person is no longer walking with a private maybe.

They are walking with a witnessed yes.

That is one of the great mercies hidden inside this doctrine.

5. Timothy's Story Opens the Door to the Full Pattern of Strengthening, Impartation, and Sending

By now, Timothy has done exactly what this chapter needs him to do.

He has carried us from hidden faithfulness...
to relational recognition...
to public confirmation...
to the formal laying on of hands passages themselves.

That is a clean biblical line.

And it matters because it helps us avoid two opposite errors.

The first error is reducing laying on of hands to mere symbolism.

The second error is treating it like spiritual magic.

Timothy gives us the middle path.

The laying on of hands is real.
It matters.
It carries weight.
It can involve prophecy, strengthening, gifting, agreement, and public confirmation.

But it is not disconnected from character.
It is not disconnected from relationship.
It is not disconnected from order.
It is not disconnected from the wider life of the person receiving it.

That is exactly why Timothy is such a strong chapter witness.

He keeps the doctrine grounded.

He keeps it human.
He keeps it relational.
He keeps it biblical.
He keeps it safe from hype.

And now that the line is clear, the chapter is ready to go deeper.

Because laying on of hands does not only recognize what God has already begun.

It can also strengthen, bless, commission, heal, impart, and send.

The hand can comfort.
The hand can confirm.
The hand can bless.
The hand can separate unto service.
The hand can stand in agreement.
The hand can become the visible point where the invisible support of God is felt.

That is where the doctrine gets even richer.

And that is where this chapter now needs to move next.

Because Timothy has shown us the recognition of the call.

The next step is to show how the church, in Scripture, does not merely *recognize* grace...

It also **releases people into assignment.**

The hand does not only say, "We see it."

Sometimes the hand also says:

Go.
Carry this.

You are not alone.
The Spirit is with you.

And that is where the doctrine of laying on of hands begins to open into commissioning, sending, and spiritual responsibility.

That is the road ahead.

And now the reader is ready for it.

Laying on of hands is not first about spectacle.
It is about recognition, agreement, and support made visible.

Timothy was not made by the moment.
He was strengthened through it.

The hand did not invent the call.
The hand helped bring it into clear and faithful order.

If Section 2 shows us **the hands that recognize the call**, then Section 3 must now show us **the hands that release people into assignment**.

Because in Scripture, laying on of hands does not stop at encouragement.

It moves into **commissioning**.

Not just, *"We see what God is doing."*
But, *"Go do what God has called you to do."*

And that is where the doctrine widens again.

SECTION 3 — THE HANDS THAT SEND

When laying on of hands moves from recognition into release

Core Scriptures:
Acts 13:2–3 (KJV)
"As they ministered to the Lord, and fasted, the Holy Ghost said, Separate me Barnabas and Saul for the work whereunto I have called them. And when they had fasted and prayed, and laid their hands on them, they sent them away."

2 Timothy 1:6 (KJV)
"Wherefore I put thee in remembrance that thou stir up the gift of God, which is in thee by the putting on of my hands."

There is a difference between being encouraged... and being entrusted.

There is a difference between someone believing in you... and the body of Christ placing hands on you and saying, *"It is time. Go."*

That is where this doctrine now moves.

In the first section, we saw the hands that support.
In the second section, we saw the hands that recognize.
But laying on of hands in Scripture does not stop at comfort or confirmation.

Sometimes the hand that blesses you... becomes the hand that sends you.

This is where the doctrine shifts from support into assignment, from recognition into release, and from being seen into being entrusted with something that now has to be carried forward **in Christ**.

And in **Acts 13**, we are given one of the clearest commissioning pictures in all of Scripture.

1. THE MOMENT WHEN SUPPORT BECOMES ASSIGNMENT

Many believers understand encouragement.
Many have felt the strength of being prayed for.
Some have even experienced the relief of being recognized by others when God has been quietly doing something in them for a long time.

But there comes another moment that feels different.

A moment when the hand is no longer simply saying, *"We are with you."*
It begins to say, *"We are releasing you."*

That can feel exciting.
It can also feel costly.

Because being loved is one thing.
Being entrusted is another.

This is where many people hesitate.

They are comfortable being supported.
They are even comforted by being affirmed.
But when the call begins to carry weight... when it begins to require movement... when it begins to ask for obedience instead of just agreement... the soul suddenly feels the cost.

That is why this part of the doctrine matters so much.

Laying on of hands is not only about blessing.
It is not only about public recognition.
Sometimes it is the visible moment where a person is
released into what God has already been forming in secret.

The hand does not always start the story.

Sometimes the hand is the green light.

2. ACTS 13 — THE CLEAN COMMISSIONING WITNESS

In **Acts 13**, the pattern is beautifully clear.

"As they ministered to the Lord, and fasted..."

Before the sending came the stillness.
Before the movement came the ministering.
Before the public release came the private posture of
worship, prayer, and fasting.

That matters.

Because true commissioning in **God's love** is not born out
of ambition.
It is born out of alignment.

This is not a man waking up and deciding he is ready
because he feels inspired.
This is not a ministry brand launch with a nice logo and a
louder microphone. 😄
This is a gathered people, ministering unto the Lord,
listening together, and waiting in the presence of God.

And then the Holy Ghost speaks:

*"Separate me Barnabas and Saul for the work whereunto I
have called them."*

That line is loaded.

The Spirit does not say, *"I am calling them right now."*
He speaks of a work **whereunto I have called them**.

In other words, the call already existed.

The laying on of hands did not invent their purpose.
It confirmed it.
It aligned the body around it.
It blessed it.
And then it released them into it.

That is one of the cleanest truths in this chapter.

**Laying on of hands does not usually create the call.
It confirms the call, strengthens the call, and sends
the call forward.**

Then the leaders respond:

*"And when they had fasted and prayed, and laid their
hands on them, they sent them away."*

That is the pattern:

1.   The Spirit speaks.
2.   The body agrees.
3.   Hands are laid on them.
4.   They are sent.
No hype.
No theatre.
No self-promotion.

Just discernment, agreement, and release.

That is the hands that send.

And this becomes the clean chapter witness for this section.

Because Barnabas and Saul show us that laying on of hands
is not merely a comforting act.
It is sometimes a commissioning act.

3. WHERE THIS SHOWS UP IN REAL LIFE

This is where the doctrine becomes personal.

Many people have experienced support.
Some have experienced recognition.
But fewer have experienced **healthy sending**.

Some were never sent.
They were simply used.

Some were pushed too early because there was a need to fill.
Some were flattered into responsibility before maturity.
Some were pressured into roles because they were available,
not because the Spirit had spoken.
And some laid hands on themselves, declared themselves
ready, and sprinted off into the bush before anyone could
ask questions. 😄

That is not Acts 13.

Acts 13 is not frantic.
It is not ego-driven.
It is not built on insecurity pretending to be zeal.

It is a deeply ordered moment in the presence of God.

That matters because many believers are not tired from
serving God.
They are tired from trying to prove a call.

They are exhausted from carrying what should have been
discerned.

They are strained from trying to force open doors that should have opened cleanly.
They are worn thin from confusing desire with commissioning.

This doctrine helps cut through that confusion.

Because the hand that sends should not push you into performance.
It should settle your heart in assignment.

When the sending is clean, the soul can settle.

Not because the road ahead is easy.
But because the heart knows:

I am not running to become something.
I am walking in what God has already spoken.

That is the difference between striving and assignment.

And this is where Timothy quietly comes back into view.

Timothy was not simply a young man who got noticed.
He was not just blessed and left standing in the glow of a meaningful moment.

He was brought into movement.

He traveled.
He learned.
He carried instruction.
He was entrusted with responsibility.
He was sent into difficult places.
He became part of the living work of God.

That means Timothy becomes proof that laying on of hands was never meant to end in a nice meeting.

It was meant to lead into mission.

4. JESUS SHOWS US WHAT CLEAN SENDING LOOKS LIKE

If Acts 13 gives us the church pattern, Jesus gives us the deeper spirit of it.

Jesus did not move by self-appointment.

He lived in continual alignment with the Father.

"For I came down from heaven, not to do mine own will, but the will of him that sent me."
— **John 6:38 (KJV)**

That is the heart beneath all true commissioning.

To live **In Christ** is not to become spiritually impressive. It is to flow in the anointed presence of **God's love** like Jesus.

And Jesus shows us that true sending is not about ego, title, or visibility.

It is about surrender, obedience, and love.

He was sent by the Father.
He moved in agreement with the Father.
He spoke what He heard.
He did what He saw.
He carried heaven into earth without self-glory.

That is the right corrective here.

Because many people want the feeling of significance...
but Jesus reveals the beauty of submission.

Many want the platform...
but Jesus reveals the power of alignment.

Many want to be known...
but Jesus shows us that the greatest strength is to be truly
sent.

This is why the doctrine of laying on of hands must stay
rooted in **God's love** and not drift into religious
performance.

The hand that sends should never send a person away from
Christ.

It should send them deeper into Him.

Not into self-importance.
Into service.

Not into image.
Into obedience.

Not into striving.
Into alignment.

That is the spirit of Acts 13.
And that is the spirit of Jesus.

5. WHAT KIND OF SENDING ARE YOU RESPONDING TO?

This is where the reader must gently locate themselves.

Not every open door is a calling.
Not every opportunity is a commission.
Not every feeling of urgency is the voice of the Spirit.

And not every delay means you are missing God.

Sometimes the holiest thing in a season is not moving faster.
It is becoming clearer.

Some readers will realize they are still in a hidden season,
and that is not failure.
God is still forming something in them.

Some will realize they have already been recognized in part,
but fear has kept them standing at the edge of obedience.

Some will realize they have been carrying a version of
"calling" that has brought more pressure than peace, more
proving than fruit, more strain than surrender.

That recognition matters.

Because this section is not here to push anyone into motion.

It is here to help the soul tell the truth.

Healthy commissioning does not inflate a person.

It steadies them.

It does not make them feel important.

It makes them available.

So before moving on, it is worth sitting quietly with a few
honest questions.

**When I think about what I am doing right now...
does it feel like I am being *sent*... or am I trying to
become?**

If what you are carrying constantly feels like you must prove
yourself, defend yourself, or force yourself into visibility,
there is a good chance your soul is trying to build an identity
instead of walking in an assignment.
But if there is a quieter kind of weight—something sober,
steady, and rooted in peace even when it feels costly—you
may be closer to true sending than you realize.

Is the thing I call "calling" drawing me deeper into obedience, humility, and God's love... or deeper into pressure, image, and strain?

The call of God may stretch you, but it should not need vanity to survive.
True commissioning in Christ does not make a person bigger in their own eyes.
It usually makes them clearer, steadier, and more willing to serve.
If what you are pursuing feeds image more than obedience, it may need to be brought back into the light.

Have I been waiting in faith... or hiding behind delay because obedience feels costly?

There is a difference between being formed and being afraid.
Some seasons are truly hidden seasons, and God is not in a rush.
But sometimes the soul uses "waiting on God" as a polite way of avoiding the next right step.
If peace keeps rising when you think about moving forward, that may be a sign that the delay is no longer protection—it may be hesitation.

Have I mistaken urgency for the Spirit... when what I really need is stillness, prayer, and clearer alignment?

Urgency can feel spiritual when the soul is under pressure.
But Acts 13 shows us a different atmosphere: ministering, fasting, listening, and then sending.
God is not confused.
He is not frantic.
And when He sends, the direction may be weighty, but it carries a different kind of clarity than panic ever can.

If trusted hands in my life prayed over what I am pursuing right now... would there be peace, or would there be hesitation?

This is not about handing your life over to human approval.
It is about humility.
Sometimes the body of Christ can see what we cannot.
Sometimes trusted people can confirm what God has already been saying.
And sometimes their hesitation is not rejection—it is mercy, protection, or a call to deeper preparation.

Support is powerful.
Recognition is powerful.
Commissioning is powerful.

But the doctrine of laying on of hands does not stop at visible agreement.

Sometimes the hand is not only sending a person forward... it is helping awaken what must sustain them when they get there.

So the next question becomes:

What exactly was Timothy told to stir up... and how did the laying on of hands relate to the gift that was in him?

SECTION 4 — THE HANDS THAT STIR THE GIFT

How what is placed in a life through God's love is not meant to remain dormant, but to be stirred into living function In Christ

Core Scriptures:
"Neglect not the gift that is in thee, which was given thee by prophecy, with the laying on of the hands of the presbytery." — 1 Timothy 4:14 (KJV)

"Wherefore I put thee in remembrance that thou stir up the gift of God, which is in thee by the putting on of my hands." — 2 Timothy 1:6 (KJV)

The life **In Christ** is often not scripted beforehand.

If it were, the soul would only get in the way.

The soul likes certainty.
It likes control.
It likes a map with the corners labeled and the risks reduced.

But the life of Christ does not usually unfold that way.

Jesus walked in continual surrender, continual listening, continual response.

He did not move as a self-generated man trying to force spiritual outcomes.
He moved as a Son in living union with the Father.

"I can of mine own self do nothing: as I hear, I judge: and my judgment is just..." — *John 5:30 (KJV)*

That is not weakness.

That is alignment.

That is what life **In Christ** actually looks like:
not scripted control,
but living responsiveness.

Not dead religious repetition.
Not self-powered ambition.
Not soul-driven performance.

But a life that listens, responds, and moves in step with the will of the Father.

And the will of the Father is not a cold list of tasks.

It is the living expression of His nature.

Mercy.
Compassion.
Patience.
Loving-kindness.
Truth.
Forgiveness.
Justice.

The flow of **Exodus 34:6**.

The life of Jesus was not random.
It was perfectly ordered by love.

That matters here, because when people hear words like *gift, impartation, activation,* or *laying on of hands,* they often drift into one of two errors:

Either they reduce it to ritual...
or they turn it into spectacle.

But the biblical pattern is simpler and deeper than both.

God places something in a life.
God confirms what He has placed.
God stirs what He has placed.
And then that life must learn to walk with Him in it.

That is what we see in Jesus with His disciples.

He calls ordinary men.
He draws them near.
He teaches them by life, not lecture alone.
He sends them before they feel fully ready.
And over time, what was first received begins to move
through them.

That is also what we see in Timothy.

He is not a celebrity story.

He is a young man of sincere faith.
Seen.
Encouraged.
Recognized.
Affirmed.
Prayed over.
Stirred.
Then slowly shaped into someone who could carry what was
entrusted to him.

And if we are reading honestly, Timothy is not just Timothy.

Timothy is the reader.

He is the ordinary believer standing in the space between:
what was recognized,

what was imparted,
and what now must be stewarded.

That is where many sincere believers get stuck.

They have had moments.
They have had prayer.
They have had tears.
They have had prophetic words.
They have had someone lay hands on them.
They have even sensed that something real happened.

But then life moved on.

And what was real in the moment was never brought into
rhythm, maturity, or stewardship.

That is why this section matters.

Because the doctrine of laying on of hands is not only about
blessing, support, or public confirmation.
It is also about **activation**.

Not the kind modern hype culture likes to market.
Not emotional electricity for its own sake.
Not a room chasing manifestations because silence feels too
ordinary.

The biblical pattern is steadier than that.

Something is given.
Something is recognized.
Something is confirmed.
And then something must be **stirred**.

That is Timothy's story.

And if we are paying attention, it may be ours too.

1. A GIFT CAN BE REAL… AND STILL GO QUIET

One of the gentlest but strongest warnings Paul gives Timothy is this:

"Neglect not the gift that is in thee…"

That line tells us something important.

A gift can be real… and still be neglected.

A calling can be genuine… and still sit dormant.

A grace can be present… and still go unused.

A deposit from God can remain in a person while daily life never fully lines up with it.

That is sobering.

And strangely comforting.

Because many sincere believers assume that if something from God were truly real, it would automatically overpower everything else.

But that is not how scripture presents maturity.

God may give.
God may speak.
God may confirm.
God may even use the laying on of hands as part of that moment.

But the one who receives still has to respond.

The gift is not a machine.
The gift is not a performance switch.
The gift is not a permanent emotional high.

It is a grace.
A trust.
A stewardship.

And stewardship requires participation.

That is why Paul does not speak to Timothy like a showman
speaking to a crowd.
He speaks like a spiritual father speaking to a son.

Not, "Prove the gift."
Not, "Impress the room."
Not, "Make sure people can feel it."

But:

Do not neglect it.

That is such a clean sentence.

It means:

- do not ignore what God has placed in you
- do not bury what was recognized over your life
- do not let fear, distraction, insecurity, or comfort
  smother what heaven intended to grow
- do not confuse delay with absence

Some things in God are not absent.

They are simply underused.

Many believers have done exactly this without realizing it.

They had a real moment with God.
A real prayer.
A real confirmation.
A real stirring.
A real encounter in God's love.

But because it did not become spectacular enough, immediate enough, or easy enough, they quietly concluded that nothing happened.

Yet scripture says otherwise.

Sometimes the issue is not whether the gift was given.

Sometimes the issue is whether it has been **neglected**.

That is why laying on of hands must be understood properly.

If we misunderstand the doctrine, we either reduce it to empty ritual or inflate it into emotional theatre.

But in scripture, it often sits in the middle like a stable bridge:
a moment where heaven touches earth, and then a life must be built around what was entrusted.

Timothy was not told to invent a gift.

He was told not to neglect the one already in him.

That is a word worth sitting with.

2. TIMOTHY'S GIFT WAS CONFIRMED IN COMMUNITY... BUT STIRRED IN PERSONAL STEWARDSHIP

By this point in the chapter, Timothy's journey is becoming clear.

He was not a random spotlight story.

He was a young man shaped by sincere faith.
He was seen by Paul.
He was strengthened through relationship.
He was publicly recognized.
He was prayed over.
He was affirmed by prophecy.
He was connected to the presbytery.
And he also carried a personal impartation linked to Paul's hands.

That is a remarkably balanced biblical picture.

In **1 Timothy 4:14**, Paul says:

"...which was given thee by prophecy, with the laying on of the hands of the presbytery."

That shows a communal moment.

There was prophetic recognition.
There was agreement.
There was a public act of laying on of hands by the elders.

This was not private imagination.

This was witnessed.
Confirmed.
Shared.

Then in **2 Timothy 1:6**, Paul says:

"...stir up the gift of God, which is in thee by the putting on of my hands."

Now the language narrows.

Paul speaks personally.

Not to contradict the first moment, but to deepen it.

The presbytery laid hands on Timothy.
Paul laid hands on Timothy.
Prophecy was involved.
Recognition was involved.
Relationship was involved.

And the result was not merely ceremony.

Something was imparted.
Something was activated.
Something was entrusted.

This is why the doctrine matters.

Because laying on of hands in scripture is often connected to:

- blessing
- identification
- healing
- commissioning
- recognition
- and sometimes **impartation**

But the Bible never treats this as magic.

It is not "hands equal power" in some mechanical sense.

It is not flesh carrying divine force like a battery pack.

It is relationship under God's order.
It is obedience inside God's love.
It is agreement with what the Spirit is doing.
It is a visible act aligning with an invisible reality.

And Timothy's story protects us from both extremes.

It protects us from the dry religious extreme that says,
"Nothing meaningful happens. It is just symbolic."

And it protects us from the sensational extreme that says, "If something meaningful happens, it must always be dramatic, immediate, and emotionally overwhelming."

Scripture gives us a steadier road.

A real gift.
A real prophetic recognition.
A real laying on of hands.
A real impartation.
A real responsibility.

That is far more useful than hype.

Because hype wants a moment.

God often wants a life.

Timothy became a chapter in the Bible not because he had one dramatic service…

…but because he stayed with what had been placed in him.

That is the difference.

3. IMPARTATION IS BIBLICAL… BUT IT WAS NEVER MEANT TO BECOME A SHOW

This is where we need clarity.

Because the moment people hear words like:

- impartation
- activation
- anointing
- laying on of hands
- stirring the gift

...many minds immediately go in one of two directions.

Either they become suspicious.

Or they become overly excited.

And both reactions can miss the truth.

The Bible does show that something real can be imparted through the laying on of hands.

Timothy is one of the clearest examples.

Paul does not merely say, "Remember the encouragement you felt."

He says:

"...the gift of God, which is in thee by the putting on of my hands."

That is stronger than symbolism alone.

Yet the same scriptures refuse to turn this into performance culture.

Paul does not coach Timothy into chasing sensations.

He does not tell him to recreate the atmosphere of the original moment.

He does not say:

- "Try to feel what you felt that night"
- "Go find another stronger touch"
- "Keep collecting experiences until your confidence returns"

Instead, he points Timothy toward something far more mature:

Stir up the gift.

That means:

- take responsibility for what has been entrusted
- exercise it
- feed it
- make room for it
- move with it
- obey where it leads
- do not let fear silence it
- do not let passivity bury it

This matters for the Body of Christ.

Because many believers have been hurt by two counterfeit patterns:

1) Empty Ritual

Hands are laid on people, but nothing is expected, nothing is taught, and nothing is stewarded.

2) Emotional Hype

Hands are laid on people, and the whole focus becomes visible reaction:
falling, shaking, shouting, intensity, atmosphere, spectacle.

Now, can God move powerfully in visible ways?

Of course.

But visible reaction is not the biblical proof of maturity.

Fruit is.

Faithfulness is.

Growth is.

Obedience is.

Love is.

A person can shake in a meeting and still neglect the gift afterward.

Another person may quietly receive a deep impartation, go home, pray, obey, endure, grow, and become a steady carrier of God's love **In Christ** for decades.

Which one looks more like Timothy?

That question answers itself.

This is why this section matters so much.

Because the doctrine of laying on of hands must be rescued from both dead religion and shallow excitement.

The real thing is holier than ritual.
And steadier than hype.

Impartation may begin in a moment.
Stewardship proves it over time.

That line is worth underlining in thick carpenter's pencil.

4. WHERE THIS SHOWS UP IN US: MANY OF US WANT THE MOMENT... BUT GOD IS BUILDING THE LIFE

This is where Timothy's story stops being "his" story and starts becoming a mirror.

Because if we are honest, most people love the moment more than the process.

We love:

- the prayer line
- the prophetic word
- the emotional breakthrough
- the goosebumps
- the tears
- the sense that something is happening

And sometimes those moments are absolutely real.

Thank God for them.

Some moments do mark us.
Some moments do shift us.
Some moments do become turning points in God's love.

But a turning point is not the same as a finished road.

That is where many believers quietly lose heart.

They receive a genuine touch from God…
but then they wake up on Tuesday.

And Tuesday is far less dramatic than Sunday.

The room is gone.
The music is gone.
The hands are gone.
The atmosphere is gone.
The encouragement is quieter.
The body still feels the same.
The soul still has habits.
Fear still whispers.
Life still demands things.

And in that ordinary place, many conclude:

"Maybe it wasn't real."

But Timothy's story says otherwise.

The gift can be real...
and still require stirring.

The impartation can be real...
and still require courage.

The moment can be real...
and still require long obedience.

This is where the doctrine becomes deeply practical.

Because many people are not lacking a touch.

They are lacking a framework.

They do not know what to do next.

They do not know how to steward what God began.

They do not know how to move from:

- experience into obedience
- confirmation into practice
- impartation into maturity
- stirring into stable fruit

And that is exactly why this book matters.

Because to live **In Christ** is not to become addicted to spiritual intensity.

It is to learn how to **flow in the anointed presence of God's love like Jesus.**

That flow may sometimes be powerful and dramatic.

But very often, it looks like:

- quiet faithfulness
- repeated obedience

- returning to prayer
- returning to truth
- using what God has placed in you
- loving people when there is no applause
- showing up when no one is watching
- speaking when the Spirit nudges
- serving when it would be easier to stay hidden

That is what stirs a gift into maturity.

And if I can step in here as a fellow traveler for a moment...

I've seen enough in life to know the difference between chaos and alignment.

As a carpenter, I worked in places where the atmosphere felt constantly noisy, pressured, and off-balance.

And I worked around Christian environments where, week after week, there would be little things—sometimes small, sometimes major—that honestly felt like miracles.

Not because everyone was floating around in clouds.

But because something in the order was different.
Something in the agreement was different.
Something in the atmosphere of God's love was different.

Things would open.
Provision would come.
Problems would shift.
Timing would align.
Peace would show up where pressure should have ruled.

That does not mean believers never face trouble.

It means there is a real difference between trying to force life in the flesh and learning to move in God's order **In Christ**.

**The gift is not meant to entertain us.
It is meant to equip us.**

And that changes everything.

5. EVALUATE: WHAT HAVE YOU BEEN GIVEN... AND WHAT HAVE YOU DONE WITH IT?

Near the end of this section, we move into guided discovery.

Not to pressure you.
Not to make you perform.
Not to drag you into self-consciousness.

But to help you recognize what may already be true.

Because many people are not waiting for a first touch from God.

They are standing on top of a neglected one.

Have there been moments in your life where something in you was clearly stirred—but over time you quietly treated it like it was nothing?
Maybe someone prayed for you.
Maybe a scripture came alive.
Maybe a burden for people grew stronger.
Maybe you sensed a gift, a direction, or a grace that felt unmistakably real in the moment.
It may not have looked dramatic on the outside, but inside you knew something shifted.
If that happened, do not rush to dismiss it just because life got noisy afterward.
Some things from God do not disappear.
They wait for stewardship.

**Are you looking for another dramatic moment...
when God may actually be asking you to stir what
has already been placed in you?**
This is where maturity often begins.
Not in chasing a stronger feeling, but in responding to what
has already been entrusted.
You may not need a new conference.
You may not need a louder room.
You may not need more hands on your head.
You may need to pray again, obey again, speak again, serve
again, trust again.
The gift often becomes clearer in use, not in observation.

**If God has placed something in you, what would it
look like this week to steward it instead of merely
admire the memory of it?**
Bring it into the ordinary.
If it is encouragement, encourage someone.
If it is prayer, pray.
If it is teaching, start sharing truth.
If it is mercy, show up for someone hurting.
If it is leadership, take responsibility where you are.
If it is discernment, slow down and listen.
The gift grows stronger when it is brought into faithful
motion inside God's love.
That is how what was stirred becomes established **In
Christ**.

That is the real question.

Not:

Did something happen?

But:

What have you done with what happened?

That is where Timothy stands as a witness.

He was not told to become spectacular.

He was told to become faithful.

And that may be one of the clearest pictures of spiritual maturity in the whole New Testament.

CLOSING ANCHOR

Jesus received from the Father and walked it out in living obedience.

The disciples received from Jesus and were sent to carry it forward.

Timothy received through prophecy, presbytery, and Paul's hands, then had to stir what was entrusted and live it.

That is the pattern.

What is given must become lived.
What is stirred must become steady.
What is received must become fruitful.

Because the hands once laid on you were never meant to end with you.

They were preparing you to become someone who can strengthen, confirm, and send others **In Christ**.

And that is where we go next.

SECTION 5 — THE HANDS THAT CARRY HIS LIFE

When God's love becomes tangible through His family In Christ

Core Scriptures:
1 Timothy 1:5 (KJV) — *"Now the end of the commandment is charity out of a pure heart, and of a good conscience, and of faith unfeigned:"*

Matthew 9:37–38 (KJV) — *"Then saith he unto his disciples, The harvest truly is plenteous, but the labourers are few; Pray ye therefore the Lord of the harvest, that he will send forth labourers into his harvest."*

1 Timothy 5:22 (KJV) — *"Lay hands suddenly on no man, neither be partaker of other men's sins: keep thyself pure."*

2 Timothy 2:2 (KJV) — *"And the things that thou hast heard of me among many witnesses, the same commit thou to faithful men, who shall be able to teach others also."*

Laying on of hands is not the end of the story.
It is often the moment people remember because it felt sacred, weighty, or marked.
But in Scripture, the hands are rarely the destination.
They are a doorway.

This doctrine is not merely about a moment in a meeting.
It is not merely about being prayed for at the front of a church.
It is not merely about receiving support, blessing, or impartation and then carrying on as if the point was the feeling.

Laying on of hands is the gift of God's love made tangible through His family In Christ.

That is what this chapter has been moving toward.

At first, the doctrine can feel abstract.
It can feel like one of those church phrases people repeat without really explaining.
But as we have walked through Timothy's life, what was abstract has become tangible.

A hand of blessing.
A hand of recognition.
A hand of confirmation.
A hand that stirs the gift.
A hand that strengthens and sends.

And now we arrive at the real question:

What is in your hands now?

Because the goal of laying on of hands was never just that someone would touch *you*.
The goal was that the life of Christ would continue to move *through* you.

1. The hands that once helped you were always meant to become the hands that help someone else

Many people spend years searching for the bigger picture while neglecting what God has already placed in their hands.

They are waiting for the perfect assignment.
Waiting for the clear title.
Waiting for the prophetic word.
Waiting for the invitation.
Waiting for the right church role.
Waiting for the grand unveiling of the will of God.

Meanwhile, the Father has already placed something in front of them.

A person to love.
A burden to help carry.
A gift to steward.
A truth to walk in.
A conversation to have.
A prayer to pray.
A need they can actually meet.

Sometimes we are so busy looking for the *future* will of God that we miss the **present** will of God.

And very often, the present will of God is where the larger call is already hiding.

I have heard many people say,
"I just don't know what the will of God is for my life."

I know that feeling.
I have felt that too.

That question can sit in the soul like a fog.
It can make a person feel uncertain, delayed, and somehow left behind.
It can make the will of God sound like a hidden map reserved for a few special people who somehow got the secret envelope.

This is one of the reasons I wrote this book.

Because when I began to understand the absolute will of God for my life, I realized it was not just for *my* life.
It was for **every life In Christ**.

The will of God is not first a private mystery about platform, title, or career.
The will of God is first a revealed way of being.

It is to live **In Christ**.
It is to **flow in the anointed presence of God's love like Jesus**.

Before the details of your assignment become clear, the direction of your life can become clear.
Before you know every place you will go, you can know the Spirit you are meant to walk in.
Before you know the scale of your calling, you can know the shape of your life.

And that changes everything.

Because if the will of God is only about some future destination, many believers will spend years feeling lost.
But if the will of God is first about becoming the kind of person who can carry His life, then the journey becomes tangible immediately.

You can begin today.
You can begin with what is already in your hands.

That is where this doctrine lands.

2. The harvest is often not waiting for more revelation — it is waiting for available hands

Jesus said the harvest is plentiful, but the labourers are few.

That is still true.

But sometimes the problem is not that there are no believers.
Sometimes the problem is that there are many believers...
and too few labourers.

Too many sitting.
Too many waiting.
Too many watching.
Too many delaying.
Too many hoping someone will finally notice what they carry.

I have seen many gifted people in church sitting quietly on their gifts, waiting to be asked.
At the very same time, I have seen pastors quietly waiting for those same people to volunteer.

That gap is more common than most people realize.

Sometimes the gap is not lack of calling.
Sometimes the gap is hesitation.

Sometimes the gap is fear.
Sometimes the gap is insecurity.
Sometimes the gap is disappointment.
Sometimes the gap is the soul waiting for certainty while love is already asking for movement.

Sometimes the gap is a believer saying,
"If they really wanted me, they would ask."

And sometimes the pastor is thinking,
"Brother... sister... the field is white already. Put your hand on the plough."

That may sound simple, but it is deeply spiritual.

Because love is not merely something we feel.
Love moves.

Love notices.
Love steps forward.
Love serves.
Love carries.
Love makes itself available.

Not because it needs applause.
Not because it needs a title.
Not because it is trying to prove itself.

But because the life of Christ naturally moves toward people.

This is why laying on of hands matters so much.

It is not just the transfer of blessing.
It is the visible reminder that the life of God often moves through **people who are willing to show up**.

The hands that carry His life are rarely the hands that wait forever to be discovered.
They are often the hands that quietly become available.

3. The proof of impartation is not sensation — it is fruit

This is where many believers get stuck.

They remember the moment.
They remember the service.
They remember the prayer line.
They remember the tears.
They remember the atmosphere.
They remember the electricity in the room.

And some of those moments are real.
Some of them are holy.
Some of them matter deeply.

But the proof of impartation is not the intensity of the moment.

The proof of impartation is fruit.

Not hype.
Not theatre.
Not how dramatic the room felt.
Not how loudly someone spoke.
Not whether your knees went weak.

Fruit.

Steady love.
Growing patience.
A cleaner conscience.
A quieter ego.
A stronger yes.
A more dependable life.
A greater burden for people.
A greater willingness to serve.
A deeper alignment with God's love In Christ.

That is what Paul kept calling Timothy toward.

Not merely, *"Remember the moment hands were laid on you."*
But also, *"Stir up the gift."*

"Be strong in the grace that is in Christ Jesus."
"Commit the same to faithful men."

In other words:

**Do not just treasure the moment.
Steward what it placed in you.**

Timothy's story is beautiful because it does not stop at recognition.

He was known.
He was affirmed.
Hands were laid on him.
A gift was stirred.
He was strengthened.
He was entrusted.
And then he was told to carry that same life forward into others.

That is not just Timothy's pattern.

That is the pattern of Christ moving through His body.

At some point, the hands that once steadied *you* become the hands that steady *someone else*.

That is the crossing.

That is the line.

That is when what once felt abstract becomes visible.

4. Love must move — but love must also be led

This is where the doctrine matures.

Because the answer is not reckless activity.
The answer is not emotional overreach.
The answer is not to start laying hands on everyone in sight
because you finally got excited.

Paul also told Timothy:

"Lay hands suddenly on no man..."

That is not a contradiction.
That is wisdom.

Love must move.
But love must also be led.

Not every need is your assignment.
Not every open door is the Spirit.
Not every emotional moment is God's direction.
Not every person is ready for your hands.
Not every burden is yours to carry.

This is where many sincere believers get tangled.

Some stay frozen and never move.
Others move too quickly and become entangled in things
God never asked them to carry.

Both can drain the soul.

This is why discernment matters.

Spirit-led boundaries are not the enemy of love.
They are often what preserve love.

God's love is not careless.
God's love is not naive.
God's love is not manipulated by every urgent voice.
God's love is merciful and gracious, yes — but it is also true,
clean, and just.

That means the mature believer learns two things at the
same time:

How to become available.
And
How to remain led.

That is a powerful combination.

Available hands.
Clear boundaries.
Warm heart.
Clean conscience.
Steady spirit.

That is not passivity.
That is maturity.

And it is exactly why this chapter must lead into the next
one.

Because the more the life of Christ rises in a person, the
more God's nature begins to govern how they move.

5. What kind of life is flowing through your hands now?

Before we leave this chapter, maybe the most important
question is not:

"Have hands ever been laid on me?"

That matters.
It is biblical.
It is beautiful.
It is powerful.

But perhaps the deeper question is:

"What kind of life is flowing through my hands now?"

Because that is where the doctrine stops being ceremonial and starts becoming visible.

Can people feel peace when you step into the room?
Can people feel safety around your spirit?
Can people feel patience where you once carried pressure?
Can people feel compassion where you once stayed distant?
Can people feel truth without condemnation?
Can people feel strength without control?

That is where this chapter naturally opens the door to the next one.

Because resurrection from the dead is not only about a future event we hope for.
It is also about the life of God overcoming deadness *now*.

Dead reactions.
Dead religion.
Dead striving.
Dead habits.
Dead identity.
Dead love.

And what rises in its place?

Mercy.
Compassion.
Patience.
Goodness.
Truth.
Forgiveness.
Justice.

In other words, what rises is the revealed nature of God.

This is why **Exodus 34:6** matters so deeply.

Because resurrection from the dead is not merely about
coming out of a grave one day.
It is about the life of God becoming visible in a human being
now.

Not just power.
Not just promise.
But nature.

Not merely gifted people.
Living people.

Not merely touched people.
Transformed people.

Not merely people who had a moment.
People who are becoming a witness.

If laying on of hands makes God's love tangible through His
family In Christ, then resurrection from the dead reveals
what that love looks like when it fully comes alive in a
person.

That is where we are going next.

Guided Discovery

**Are you waiting for a bigger call while neglecting
what God has already placed in your hands?**

Sometimes the soul imagines the will of God as something
far away because it feels safer to chase mystery than to
embrace present responsibility.
But very often, the next step in God's will is already sitting
in front of you.

A person to love.
A gift to use.
A need to meet.
A burden to help carry.
The larger call is often hiding inside the small faithful yes.

**Are you waiting to be asked, while the harvest is
already asking for your hands?**

There are seasons when a person truly does need
recognition, confirmation, and sending.
That is biblical.
But there are also seasons when the field is already white,
the need is already obvious, and the Spirit is simply waiting
for willing hands.
Not every step requires a spotlight.
Sometimes the most anointed move is quiet availability.

Is your love both available and led?

Some believers stay frozen and never move.
Others move so quickly they become tangled in assignments
God never gave them.
Mature love learns both movement and restraint.
It knows how to step forward without becoming reckless.
It knows how to care without being consumed.
It knows how to remain warm-hearted, Spirit-led, and clean
in conscience.

Section Anchor

The hands were never meant to end at the moment of
contact.
They were meant to become carriers of the life of Christ.

If this chapter has shown us how God's love becomes
tangible through His family In Christ, the next chapter will
show us what that love looks like when it begins to fully rise
inside a person.

Not just in ministry.
Not just in moments.
Not just in meetings.

In nature.

In response.
In character.
In relationships.
In the daily walk.

Because resurrection from the dead is not only something we wait for at the end.

It is also the evidence of God's life overcoming what used to be dead in us.

And when that life rises, it begins to look like the God who revealed Himself to Moses:

Merciful.
Gracious.
Longsuffering.
Abundant in goodness and truth.

That is not just a description of God.
It is the shape of resurrection life **In Christ**.

And that is where we go next.

CHAPTER 5 — RESURRECTION FROM THE DEAD

When the Life of God Rises in You

"Of the doctrine of baptisms, and of laying on of hands, and of resurrection of the dead..."
— Hebrews 6:2 (KJV)

**"And the LORD passed by before him, and proclaimed, The LORD, The LORD God, merciful and gracious, longsuffering, and abundant in goodness and truth,
Keeping mercy for thousands, forgiving iniquity and transgression and sin, and that will by no means clear the guilty..."**
— Exodus 34:6–7 (KJV)

"Likewise reckon ye also yourselves to be dead indeed unto sin, but alive unto God through Jesus Christ our Lord."
— Romans 6:11 (KJV)

When many hear the words *resurrection from the dead*, their thoughts rush straight to the end—to graves opening, to the dead in Christ rising, to being caught up together to meet the Lord in the air. And that hope is real.

It is glorious. It is part of the great promise held before every believer.

But resurrection is more than being caught up with those in Christ to meet Jesus in the clouds.

It is also **finding that resurrection now**—while your feet are still on the earth, while your soul is still learning to yield, and while the life of God is still pressing gently against all that in you has not yet fully come alive.

It is possible to believe in the promise of resurrection while still living buried beneath old patterns in the present.

It is possible to speak the language of salvation while never pressing into the life it was meant to awaken.

Many have been taught to look ahead, but not enough have been taught how to recognize the life of God rising within them now. Yet the doctrine of Christ does not merely prepare us for a day to come. It invites us into a life that can begin to rise today.

Resurrection, then, is not only the promise that we will live after death. It is the promise that **the life of God can begin rising in us before death ever comes**.

It is the slow and holy overturning of the old man. It is **mercy** rising where judgment once rushed in. **Compassion** rising where indifference once sat. **Patience** rising where irritation once ruled. **Loving-kindness** rising where love once remained hidden. **Truth** rising where illusion once comforted. **Forgiveness** rising where pain once built a throne. **Justice rising** where compromise once stood guard.

This is resurrection as more than event. This is... **resurrection as life.**

And this is why this chapter must bring us to one of the most important revelations in all of Scripture: **Exodus 34:6–7**. When the Lord passed before Moses and declared His own name, He revealed the inner shape of His nature.

Not first power. Not first spectacle. Not first mystery. But mercy. Compassion. Patience. Loving-kindness. Truth. Forgiveness. Justice. This is not merely a list of divine qualities to admire from a distance. This is the revealed nature of the Father—and in Christ, it becomes the very pattern of the life rising in His people.

Resurrection is not merely that something dead stands up again. It is that **the life of the Father becomes visible in the child**.

And we are not left to imagine what that looks like. We have been given Jesus. Not only as the One who rose from the grave, but as the One who walked among men already full of resurrection life before the stone was ever rolled away.

In this chapter, we will not merely study the doctrine from a distance. We will walk with **the Firstborn from the dead**. We will watch what rises in Him when the broken draw near, when the proud resist, when the weak fail, when the suffering cry out, when truth must be spoken, when forgiveness must be extended, and when justice must stand.

In Jesus, resurrection begins to put on skin.

So we will move through this chapter slowly and honestly. We will begin by widening the doctrine beyond the distant horizon and bringing it close enough to touch.

Then we will look to Jesus—the Firstborn from the dead—as the first full revelation of resurrection life.

From there, He will lead us through the inner nature of the risen life, the visible fruit of the risen life, and the mature government of the risen life. And by the time we reach the end, the question will no longer be only, *Do I believe in resurrection?* It will be something deeper, quieter, and much harder to escape:

Chapter 5 Sections

1. Resurrection Is Not Only Later

This opening section gently widens the doctrine beyond the distant future. It shows that resurrection is not only a promise waiting at the end of the road, but a life that begins to rise in us here and now.

2. Jesus: The Firstborn from the Dead

This section anchors the chapter in Jesus as the first full and final revelation of resurrection life. Not merely one brought back from temporary death, but the One who was crucified, pierced, buried, sealed in a tomb, and raised in irreversible victory. From this point forward, we do not merely study resurrection life—we walk with the Firstborn through it.

3. The Inner Nature of Resurrection Life

(Mercy, Compassion, and Patience)
Here Jesus leads us into the first movements of resurrection life. We watch what rises in Him toward the broken, the slow, the suffering, and the still-forming. In His mercy, compassion, and patience, the inner posture of the Father begins to come into view.

4. The Visible Fruit of Resurrection Life

(Loving-Kindness)
Here Jesus shows us what resurrection looks like when it steps out into the world and touches real people. Loving-kindness is given room to breathe as the visible fruit of mercy, compassion, and patience working together in living form.

5. The Mature Government of Resurrection Life

(Truth, Forgiveness, and Justice)
This final section brings resurrection life into stable, mature expression. Here Jesus leads us through truth, forgiveness, and justice—not as competing forces, but as the strong and dependable government of God's love. This becomes the chapter's final threshold, and the perfect bridge into **eternal judgment**.

SECTION 1 — RESURRECTION IS NOT ONLY LATER

The promise of the future begins as the pattern of life now.

Core Scriptures:
Hebrews 6:1–2 (KJV)
"Therefore leaving the principles of the doctrine of Christ, let us go on unto perfection... Of the doctrine of baptisms, and of laying on of hands, and of resurrection of the dead, and of eternal judgment."

John 11:25 (KJV)
"Jesus said unto her, I am the resurrection, and the life..."

Romans 6:4 (KJV)
"...even so we also should walk in newness of life."

Resurrection from the dead is often spoken of as something waiting for us at the end.
A future event.
A final trumpet.
A promised rising.

And that future hope is real.
It is holy.
It must not be diminished.

The dead in Christ shall rise.
Those who belong to Him will be gathered to Him.
The promise of bodily resurrection is not poetry, and it is not religious comfort language.
It is part of the victory of Jesus Christ Himself.

But if resurrection is only ever spoken of as *later*, many believers quietly settle for a Christianity that never fully comes alive *now*.

They learn the language of salvation.
They know the phrases.
They can speak of heaven, grace, forgiveness, eternal life, and being born again.

Yet many still live inwardly pinned beneath the same fears, same reactions, same wounds, same self-protections, and same old patterns that ruled them before they ever said they believed.

It is possible to rest in the language of salvation while never pressing into the life it was meant to awaken.

That is why this doctrine appears here in Hebrews 6.
Not as a side note.
Not as a distant comfort only.
But as part of the foundation that moves the believer forward into maturity.

Resurrection from the dead is not only the promise that one day your body will rise.
It is also the declaration that the life of God was meant to begin overcoming death *in you now.*

Not merely physical death at the end of the age—
but the smaller deaths that cling to the soul in this age:

- the death of hope
- the death of courage
- the death of tenderness
- the death of trust
- the death of wonder
- the death that comes from living too long in fear, shame, striving, or survival

Many people are waiting for a resurrection event while resisting a resurrection pattern.

But the doctrine of Christ does not merely prepare you to die well.
It teaches you how to live *raised.*

This is why Paul does not only speak about resurrection as future glory.
He speaks about walking in **newness of life**.
He speaks about being **raised with Christ**.
He speaks about the old man being crucified so that something new can actually emerge.
Not just in doctrine.
In disposition.
In desire.
In daily life.

The invitation is deeper than, *"Will you go to heaven one day?"*
The invitation is also, *"Will the life of Christ begin to rise in you now?"*

That is where this chapter must begin.

Because resurrection from the dead is not first about
escaping the earth. It is about the life of heaven entering the
believer so deeply that what was once ruled by death begins
to bow to the nature of God.

This is why we will not treat resurrection here as abstract
theology.
We will honor the future resurrection fully.
But we will also press into the present reality of resurrection
life— the visible nature of God rising in the believer.

And that is where this chapter becomes deeply personal.

Because every one of us knows what it feels like to carry
areas that still feel buried.
Places where faith has language, but life has not yet caught
up.
Places where we say *"I believe,"* but still react as though
death has the final word.

This section is not here to condemn that.
It is here to uncover it gently.

Because the gospel is not ashamed to meet us in unfinished
places.

That is exactly where resurrection likes to work.

And before we move into the life that resurrection produces
in us, we must first fix our eyes where the doctrine itself
begins:

Not with an experience.
Not with a system.
Not with a theological argument.

But with a Person.

Because the only man in human history to be truly, fully, undeniably resurrected from the dead is Jesus Christ.

Not revived.
Not merely restored for a little while.
Not resuscitated back into the same mortal cycle.

Crucified.
Pierced.
Buried.
Sealed behind stone.

And still the love of God came through.

He is not only the proof that resurrection is real.
He is the pattern, the source, and the first opening in the wall.

He is **the Firstborn from the dead**.

And if this doctrine is going to become more than future language for us, it must begin where all true resurrection begins—

with **Jesus.**

1. Resurrection must be honored in both directions

If we only preach resurrection as something already experienced, we risk flattening the future hope of the gospel.

If we only preach resurrection as something far away, we risk leaving believers spiritually asleep while they wait.

The doctrine of Christ does both.

It says:
Yes — there is a coming resurrection.

And it also says:
Yes — resurrection life begins now.

The future resurrection is the full harvest.
The present resurrection life is the firstfruits.

One is not the enemy of the other.
One confirms the other.

2. Salvation language is not the same as awakened life

Many believers sincerely love Jesus, yet still live trapped in inner patterns that do not reflect His life.

That does not mean their confession is fake.
It means their formation may be unfinished.

A person can know the vocabulary of faith while still living from:

- fear instead of trust
- striving instead of surrender
- numbness instead of tenderness
- reaction instead of peace
- self-protection instead of love

This is why the doctrine must move deeper than words.

Because Christ did not come only to give us correct statements.
He came to bring us into living union.

Not merely saved *from* something.
But awakened *into* Someone.

3. Resurrection life shows up before the grave

If resurrection only matters after death, then much of the New Testament becomes strangely overbuilt.

But the apostles write as though resurrection is already invading ordinary life.

They speak of:

- **newness of life**
- **putting off the old man**
- **putting on the new man**
- **being transformed**
- **being renewed**
- **Christ in you**
- **the life of Jesus made manifest in our mortal flesh**

That is not just cemetery language.
That is discipleship language.

Resurrection begins wherever death loses its grip.

When bitterness loosens.
When shame no longer governs.
When fear stops driving.
When love becomes stronger than self-preservation.
When truth becomes more precious than image.
When patience outlives irritation.
When mercy interrupts judgment.

That is not the final resurrection.
But it is certainly the fragrance of it.

4. The unfinished places are not disqualifications

Some readers may feel a quiet ache here.

You believe in Christ.
You have walked with Him.
Yet there are still places in you that do not feel very "raised."

Old grief.
Old defense patterns.
Old reflexes.
Old weariness.
Old hidden graves.

That is not proof the doctrine has failed.

It may simply be proof that resurrection is still working.

Jesus does some of His best work in sealed places.
He is not intimidated by stones.
He is not offended by process.
And He is not confused by the places where your heart still feels late.

The question is not whether you are finished.

The question is whether you are willing to keep opening those places to the life of Christ.

5. Resurrection begins with the Firstborn

Before resurrection becomes a pattern in us, it must first be seen perfectly in Him.

We do not begin this doctrine by staring at ourselves.
We begin by looking at Jesus.

He is the first fully revealed victory over death.
He is the first true Man to pass through death and emerge
beyond its claim.
He is the firstborn from the dead.
The firstfruits.
The pattern.
The guarantee.

Everything this chapter will say about mercy, compassion,
patience, loving-kindness, truth, forgiveness, and justice will
only make sense if it is first seen in Him.

Because resurrection is not just power.
It is the life of God revealed in the face of Jesus Christ.

And if that life is now in us by the Spirit, then resurrection is
not only our future destination.

It is our present calling.

DISCOVERY — THE QUESTIONS PEOPLE OFTEN FEEL BUT DON'T ALWAYS ASK

**1. If I already believe in Jesus, why do parts of me
still feel so unchanged?**
Because belief can be real while formation is still unfolding.
The presence of unfinished places does not mean Christ is
absent.
It often means He is inviting you deeper than agreement
into transformation.

**2. Am I dishonoring the future resurrection if I talk
about resurrection life now?**
No.
You are honoring the full shape of the gospel.
The future resurrection remains a holy certainty, and

present resurrection life is its early witness already at work
in the believer.

3. What does resurrection life actually look like in everyday life?

It looks like death losing influence.
Fear loosening.
Love strengthening.
Truth stabilizing.
Mercy softening you without making you weak.
It looks like Christ becoming visible where the old you once
ruled without challenge.

Section Anchor

**Resurrection from the dead is not only the promise
that we will rise with Christ one day.
It is the invitation for the life of Christ to begin
rising in us now.**

**And before that life can be traced in us, it must first
be seen in the One who opened the way.**

Before we study resurrection as a pattern in the believer,
we must behold resurrection as a finished reality in the Son.

Because the doctrine does not begin with what we are
becoming.
It begins with who He already is.

SECTION 2 — JESUS, THE FIRSTBORN FROM THE DEAD

He did not simply come back. He came through death as the beginning of a new creation.

Core Scripture:
Colossians 1:18 (KJV) — *"And he is the head of the body, the church: who is the beginning, the firstborn from the dead; that in all things he might have the preeminence."*

There is a difference between someone being restored to natural life and someone passing through death into a new order of life altogether.

That difference matters.

Jesus did not merely recover from suffering. He did not simply wake up again. He did not return to continue the same kind of life He had before, as though resurrection were only a divine reset button. What happened in Christ was greater than recovery. Greater than survival. Greater than reversal.

He passed through death and emerged as the beginning of something entirely new.

That is why Scripture speaks of Him with such weight. He is not only the crucified One. He is not only the risen One. He is **the firstborn from the dead**. He is **the firstfruits**. He is **the beginning**. In Him, resurrection is no longer just an event to admire later. It becomes a Person to behold now.

And that changes the whole chapter.

Because resurrection from the dead is not first presented to us as a doctrine to study from a distance. It is first revealed to us in Jesus Himself. Before resurrection becomes our hope, it is His reality. Before it becomes our promise, it is His victory. Before it becomes something we long for, it is Someone we look at.

So this section slows us down and fixes our eyes on Him.

1. He Was Not Revived Back Into the Old Order

Some in Scripture were raised, but Jesus was resurrected.

That distinction is worth protecting.

Lazarus came back into mortal life and would one day die again. The widow's son was restored. Jairus' daughter was restored. These were glorious signs of God's power, and they mattered deeply, but they were not yet the full unveiling of resurrection in its highest sense.

Jesus was not raised merely to resume breathing in the same old human order.

He was crucified.
He was pierced.
He truly died.
He was laid in a tomb.
A stone was rolled across the entrance as if rock could restrain the purpose of God.
The powers of darkness spent themselves against Him.
The world treated Him as finished.

But love was not finished.

When the Father raised the Son, He did not simply return Him to ordinary biological existence. He brought Him through death into resurrection life. Not delayed death. Not interrupted death. Defeated death.

This is why the language of Scripture becomes so specific. Jesus is not described as one who merely came back. He is called **the firstborn from the dead**. The wording itself refuses reduction. It tells us that something began in Him that had never happened before in that way.

Death did not spit Him back out unchanged.
He came through it carrying the victory of a new creation.

And because He did, death is no longer the same enemy it once appeared to be.
It still intimidates the soul.
It still casts a long shadow across human fear.
But in Christ, its final authority has been broken.

Jesus did not survive death.
He overcame it.

2. The Firstborn Means the Beginning, Not Merely the Earliest

Paul does not use the language of "firstborn" casually.

In **Colossians 1:18**, Jesus is called *"the beginning, the firstborn from the dead."* Those two phrases belong together. He is not simply the first in a sequence. He is the beginning of a whole new order.

That is vital.

Biblically, firstborn carries more than timing. It carries rank, inheritance, preeminence, and representative headship. The firstborn opens the way. The firstborn stands at the front of the family line. The firstborn carries significance for those who follow.

So when Jesus is called the firstborn from the dead, Scripture is telling us that His resurrection was not an isolated miracle floating by itself in history. It was the opening of the door. The establishing of a pattern. The emergence of the true Man in full victory through the will of the Father.

He went first.

Not first merely so we could admire Him from a distance, but first so that those **in Christ** would understand the kind of life they are being called into.

This is why **Revelation 1:5** also names Him *"the first begotten of the dead."* Heaven itself keeps this language in view. It is as though the Spirit does not want us reducing the resurrection to inspiration alone. He wants us to see its order, its supremacy, and its consequences.

Jesus stands in preeminence because no one else has ever done what He did in the fullness that He did it.

He did not overcome death for Himself alone.
He overcame it as the Head of the body.

And that means resurrection is not disconnected from the church. It is not disconnected from the believer. It is not disconnected from the life now being formed in those who belong to Him.

The Head has risen.
So the body cannot think of resurrection as foreign territory.

3. He Is the Firstfruits of What Is to Follow

Paul strengthens the picture in **1 Corinthians 15:20**:
"But now is Christ risen from the dead, and become the firstfruits of them that slept."

Firstborn.
First begotten.
Firstfruits.

The thread is deliberate.

Firstfruits means the first part of the harvest that reveals what the rest is going to be like. It is the early evidence that the full yield is coming. It is not the whole harvest, but it carries the truth of the harvest inside it.

So Christ's resurrection is not only proof that He conquered death. It is also the unveiling of what God intends beyond Him for all who are His.

That does not reduce Jesus. It magnifies Him.

Because the firstfruits are holy, the rest of the harvest is interpreted through them.
Because the Head has risen, the body now has its reference point.
Because the beginning has appeared, the end is no longer a mystery of terror for those in Him.

And this reaches further than later.

Yes, the final resurrection matters.
Yes, the future bodily hope is real.
Yes, the grave will not have the last word over those who belong to Christ.

But the firstfruits principle also whispers something present and alive:
what appeared in fullness in Him is now meant to begin appearing in measure in us.

Not that we become Him.
Not that we replace Him.
Not that we imitate resurrection with religious language while remaining inwardly unchanged.

But that His life begins to press its way into ours.

The fruit appears first in Him.
Then the life of that fruit begins to work through the field.

That is where this chapter is headed.

4. Resurrection Is Revealed First in a Man Fully Aligned With the Father

When we look at Jesus, we are not only looking at power over death. We are looking at life fully yielded to the Father before death was ever overcome publicly.

His resurrection did not arrive as a random display. It was the full unveiling of a life already lived in union, obedience, surrender, truth, love, and holy agreement with the Father.

That matters because resurrection is not magic.
It is not spectacle.
It is not an isolated burst of divine energy disconnected from the nature of God.

Jesus lived in the flow of the Father's heart.

He walked in mercy.
He moved in compassion.
He carried patience with the weak, the broken, and the slow to understand.

He embodied loving-kindness.
He spoke truth without compromise.
He released forgiveness even in agony.
He trusted the justice of God without taking darkness into
His own hands.

In other words, the resurrection did not contradict the way
He lived.
It vindicated it.

The Father did not raise a stranger to His own nature.
He raised the Son who had perfectly revealed Him.

And this is where the chapter begins to turn toward us.

Because if resurrection is the life of God triumphing in
Christ, then the shape of that life is not hidden. We have
already seen it. We saw it in Jesus. We saw it in the way He
loved. We saw it in the way He endured. We saw it in the
way He responded under pressure. We saw it in the way He
kept giving the Father a body to live through.

So resurrection life is not less than power, but it is certainly
more than power.

It is the life of God made visible in a human being.

Jesus is the firstborn from the dead, and in Him we are
shown not only that death can be conquered, but what
conquered humanity actually looks like.

5. The Firstborn Now Leads Us Into Resurrection Life, Not Mere Resurrection Language

This is where many believers have unconsciously settled for
too little.

They honor the resurrection.
They sing about the resurrection.
They defend the resurrection.
They build doctrine around the resurrection.
They wait for the resurrection.

But they do not always recognize that the Firstborn is also leading His people into resurrection life now.

It is possible to celebrate that Jesus rose while resisting the kind of inward dying that makes room for His life to be formed in us.

It is possible to rejoice in the empty tomb while still clinging to the old man's reactions, the old wounds, the old patterns, the old self-protective instincts, and the old definitions of life.

It is possible to believe in resurrection as a future event while avoiding resurrection as a present invasion.

But Jesus did not rise merely to improve our theology.
He rose to become preeminent.

And where He is given preeminence, things begin to change.

His mercy begins to confront our hardness.
His compassion begins to interrupt our indifference.
His patience begins to outlast our irritations.
His loving-kindness begins to soften the edges of our living.
His truth begins to steady what is crooked.
His forgiveness begins to release what we keep carrying.
His justice begins to defend what is good and put boundaries around what destroys.

That is not another gospel.
That is the life of the risen Christ pressing into the believer.

The firstborn from the dead is not absent from His body.
He is the Head of it.

And the Head is not dead.
The Head is alive.

So this section does not leave us staring only at a tomb
behind us or a trumpet before us.
It leaves us with Jesus Himself—alive, preeminent, first, and
leading.

He is not only the proof that resurrection exists.
He is the pattern of what resurrection life looks like when
the Father has room to live again in man.

Guided Discovery

1. What makes Jesus' resurrection different from every other raising in Scripture?

Others were restored to mortal life, but Jesus came through
death into a new order of life. He was not merely returned to
the old world. He emerged as the firstborn from the dead—
the beginning of a new creation pattern in the purpose of
God.

2. Why does Scripture call Him the firstborn and firstfruits?

Because His resurrection is not an isolated miracle. It is the
opening of the way. He stands first in preeminence, and
what appeared fully in Him becomes the pattern, promise,
and living reference point for those who are in Christ.

3. If Jesus is the firstborn from the dead, what does that mean for my life now?

It means resurrection is not only something to believe in
later. It is a life to yield to now. The risen Christ is not
calling you merely to admire His victory, but to let His life

begin to rise in you—through mercy, compassion, patience, loving-kindness, truth, forgiveness, and justice.

Jesus did not simply return from death.
He passed through it as the Firstborn, the Firstfruits, and the Beginning.

And if the Beginning now lives in His people, then resurrection from the dead cannot remain only a future promise.
It must begin to show itself as a present life.

That is where we now turn.

Because the life that conquered death in Christ has a recognizable nature.
And that nature begins to appear wherever the risen life of God takes form in us.

SECTION 3 — MERCY, COMPASSION, AND PATIENCE

The first visible movements of resurrection life are not power displays, but the nature of God rising in us through Christ.

Core Scripture:
Exodus 34:6 (KJV) — *"And the Lord passed by before him, and proclaimed, The Lord, The Lord God, merciful and gracious, longsuffering, and abundant in goodness and truth."*

Resurrection from the dead is not only the promise that we will live after the grave. It is the beginning of God's own life rising in us now. Before resurrection is seen in glory, it begins to show itself in nature.

Before it is revealed in immortality, it is revealed in character. Before it is seen in the body, it begins to move through the heart.

This is why Exodus 34:6 matters so deeply here. If resurrection life is the life of Christ in us, then it must begin where His life begins to become visible.

Not first in noise.

Not first in reputation.

Not first in gifts that impress the soul.

But in mercy, compassion, and patience.

Jesus did not rise from the dead merely to prove He had power over death. He rose as the firstborn from the dead so that His life could begin to appear in His people.

The first signs of that life are often quieter than many expect. A harder man becomes softer. A harsh woman becomes gentler. A reactive heart begins to slow down. Judgment loosens its grip. Space is made for people to grow. Love no longer needs to win every moment. That is resurrection life beginning to breathe.

These are not small things. They are the early movements of a new creation.

1. Mercy is love choosing not to crush

Mercy is often easiest to understand in a courtroom. Someone is guilty. The facts are clear. The authority to judge is real. Yet instead of giving the full weight of what could be given, mercy restrains the blow.

That is why mercy is such a beautiful beginning point for resurrection life.

It reveals strength under control. Mercy is not weakness pretending to be kind. **Mercy is kindness from a position of authority or right standing**.

It is love with the power to strike, choosing instead to hold back for a greater purpose.

Jesus embodied this everywhere He went. He did not walk through the earth looking for reasons to condemn. He walked through the earth carrying the heart of the Father. The woman caught in adultery stood in the blast zone of law, shame, and public exposure. Men were ready with stones.

Yet Jesus did not deny the seriousness of sin, and He did not join the frenzy of destruction either. He brought the room back under truth, and then He released mercy into it.

John 8:10–11 (KJV) — ***"When Jesus had lifted up himself, and saw none but the woman, he said unto her, Woman, where are those thine accusers? hath no man condemned thee? She said, No man, Lord. And Jesus said unto her, Neither do I condemn thee: go, and sin no more."***

That is not softness without direction. That is mercy with a doorway forward.

Resurrection life begins to show in us when we stop needing to crush people for being unfinished. When someone fails, stumbles, reacts badly, or exposes weakness, the old man often wants to strike quickly. The soul enjoys superiority more than it admits. But resurrection life does not feed on another person's collapse. It looks for the redemptive opening.

Mercy says, *I see the failure, but I also see the person.*
Mercy says, *I could push harder here, but love is calling for wisdom.*
Mercy says, *This moment does not have to end in destruction.*

That is not human niceness. That is Christ rising in His people.

2. Compassion is love moved by another's suffering

If mercy restrains judgment, compassion moves toward pain.

Compassion is not mere pity. Pity can stand at a distance and feel sorry for someone without moving. Compassion comes closer. It feels the suffering and wants to help. It is the heart of love stirred into movement.

Jesus was constantly moved this way.

Matthew 14:14 (KJV) — ***"And Jesus went forth, and saw a great multitude, and was moved with compassion toward them, and he healed their sick."***

Mark 6:34 (KJV) — ***"And Jesus, when he came out, saw much people, and was moved with compassion toward them, because they were as sheep not having a shepherd: and he began to teach them many things."***

Notice how compassion in Jesus was not selective to one kind of need. Sometimes it healed. Sometimes it fed.

Sometimes it taught. Sometimes it restored dignity. Sometimes it stopped long enough to see the one person everyone else had learned to step around.

This matters because many people imagine resurrection life mainly in terms of spiritual intensity.

But Jesus shows us something more dependable. The risen life is not less tender than the earthly life of Jesus. It is more fully established in it.

The One who rose from the dead is the same One who stopped for the blind, touched the leper, fed the hungry, and wept with the grieving.

So when compassion begins to rise in us, resurrection is no longer only a doctrine we believe. It is becoming a life we carry.

Compassion changes the way we see people.
It slows down the impatient glance.
It interrupts the convenience of self-focus.
It asks, *What is this person carrying?*
It asks, *What would love do here?*
It asks, *Is there some way to lighten this load?*

In Christ, compassion is not an optional personality trait for the naturally soft-hearted. It is part of the visible nature of God. Some may express it more openly than others, but all resurrection life bends this way.

A heart that cannot be moved eventually becomes dangerous, even if its doctrine is correct.

3. Patience is love making room for growth

Patience is where mercy and compassion learn how to stay.

Anyone can have a brief emotional moment. Anyone can feel stirred for a second. But patience is what allows love to endure long enough for transformation to happen. Patience gives time for repentance, growth, and change.

This is why Exodus 34:6 does not merely say God is merciful and gracious. It also says He is **longsuffering**.

He is not only good in a moment. He remains good across time. He does not give up at the first resistance, the first delay, the first confusion, or the first immaturity.

This too was visible in Jesus.

Think of the disciples. How often did they misunderstand Him? How often did they reach for rank, react in fear, speak too quickly, or fail to discern what was right in front of them? Yet Jesus kept walking with them.

He corrected them, but He did not discard them. He confronted them, but He did not abandon them. He stayed with them long enough for truth to settle, for failure to expose them, and for love to reshape them.

That is patience.

Resurrection life is patient because it is not insecure. It does not need instant visible success to feel justified. It knows what it is building.

The soul hates patience because patience feels like loss of control. It wants quick outcomes, immediate proof, and tidy conclusions. But love understands process.

Love knows that some fruit only grows in season. Love knows that people do not always change at the speed of our discomfort.

Patience does not mean removing boundaries. It does not mean pretending nothing matters. It does not mean enabling damage or refusing truth. It means that love is strong enough to remain rightly positioned while time does its work.

Patience says, *I will not panic because you are still growing.*
Patience says, *I do not need to force what only truth and time can form.*
Patience says, *I will keep standing in what is right without becoming hard-hearted.*

This is one of the clearest signs that resurrection life is becoming real in someone. They no longer need everything to happen immediately. They can remain anchored in God's nature while life unfolds.

4. These three movements prepare the way for the rest of God's nature

Mercy, compassion, and patience are not random virtues floating beside one another. They work together. They are the opening atmosphere of resurrection life.

Mercy stops love from becoming cruel.
Compassion stops love from becoming cold.
Patience stops love from becoming shallow.

Together, they prepare the way for loving-kindness to become visible. Together, they create the inner climate where truth can be received without becoming a weapon. Together, they make forgiveness possible without cheapening justice.

This is why this chapter does not rush straight into power language. The resurrection of Jesus is the highest victory in human history, but the life that flows from that victory does not first appear as spectacle. It appears as the nature of God becoming increasingly visible in His people.

The greatest miracle may not be that a man can speak in power.
It may be that he no longer needs to dominate.
The greatest miracle may not be that a woman can move mountains.
It may be that she now carries mercy where bitterness once lived.
The greatest miracle may not be what appears on a platform.
It may be what has quietly risen in the hidden places of the heart.

This is resurrection beginning to take shape.

5. Jesus is not only our example here — He is our life

We must be careful not to turn this section into moral advice. This is not a chapter saying, *Try harder to be merciful, compassionate, and patient.* If left there, it would become another dead work chapter dressed in prettier clothes.

The point is deeper.

Jesus, the firstborn from the dead, is not only showing us what resurrection looks like. He is the source of resurrection life itself. He does not merely stand ahead of us as an example we strain to imitate. He comes to us as life to be received, trusted, and formed in us.

Galatians 2:20 (KJV) — *"I am crucified with Christ: nevertheless I live; yet not I, but Christ liveth in me..."*

That changes everything.

Mercy is no longer just something we should offer. It becomes the mercy of Christ rising through us.
Compassion is no longer just emotional sensitivity. It becomes the heart of Christ moving through us.
Patience is no longer gritted-teeth restraint. It becomes the steadiness of Christ teaching us to remain.

So the question of resurrection is not only, *Do you believe Jesus rose?*
It is also, **Is His risen life beginning to appear in you?**

That question is not meant to condemn the sincere believer. It is meant to awaken hunger. Because once you see that resurrection is not only later but now, you start looking for its movements differently.

You stop measuring life only by outward intensity. You begin to watch for the nature of God taking form in the ordinary places where real discipleship happens.

And often, that is where Jesus is nearest.

Guided Discovery

1. Where in your life are you being invited to show mercy instead of judgment?

Sometimes the clearest sign that Christ is rising in us is not that we know what is wrong, but that we no longer need to strike with it. Mercy does not deny truth. It simply refuses to use truth as a hammer when love is calling for a doorway.

2. Who around you may need compassion more than correction right now?

Not every struggle is solved by sharper words. Some people do need truth, but they need it carried by a heart that has taken time to see their pain. Jesus often helped people before He explained them.

3. What situation is teaching you patience — not passive delay, but steady love under God?
Patience is one of the hardest proofs of resurrection life because it forces the soul to surrender control. Yet often this is where the deepest formation happens. Love stays rightly positioned long enough for growth to occur.

Directional Lances

- Resurrection life begins to show itself in the visible nature of God.
- Mercy, compassion, and patience are the first movements of that life.
- Jesus did not only model these things; He now lives them in us.
- The risen life is not proved only by power displayed, but by God's nature becoming visible.
- What rises first in Christ is often not spectacle, but love under pressure.

SECTION 4 — LOVING-KINDNESS

When Mercy, Compassion, and Patience Become Visible

Core Scripture:
Exodus 34:6 (KJV) — *"And the Lord passed by before him, and proclaimed, The Lord, The Lord God, merciful and gracious, longsuffering, and abundant in goodness and truth."*

Secondary Witnesses:
Psalm 63:3 (KJV) — *"Because thy lovingkindness is better than life, my lips shall praise thee."*

Ephesians 2:4–7 (KJV) — *"But God, who is rich in mercy, for his great love wherewith he loved us... hath raised us up together..."*

John 3:17 (KJV) — *"For God sent not his Son into the world to condemn the world; but that the world through him might be saved."*

Loving-kindness is what mercy looks like when it stays.
It is what compassion looks like when it moves.
It is what patience looks like when it keeps showing up.

This is why loving-kindness is not merely a feeling.
It is not vague niceness.
It is not weak tolerance pretending to be holy.

Loving-kindness is love made visible.
It is the nature of God becoming recognizable in action.

And if resurrection from the dead is not only a future event but the life of God rising in the believer now, then loving-kindness is one of the clearest signs that something has already come alive inside you.

Jesus did not only speak about the Father's heart.
He embodied it.
He walked it into rooms.
He touched it into people.
He held it steady under pressure.
And what people felt around Him was not merely power.
It was the kindness of God with backbone.

That is the doorway of this section.

1. LOVING-KINDNESS IS LOVE WITH FORM

Mercy chooses not to crush.
Compassion feels the suffering.
Patience makes room for change.

But loving-kindness is where all three stop being internal
and begin to take shape.

It is the visible fruit of mercy, compassion, and patience
working together.

This matters because many believers know how to agree
with God in principle but do not yet know how to reflect
Him in pattern.

They may believe God is loving.
They may even preach that God is loving.
But when pressure comes, interruption comes,
disappointment comes, people still receive sharpness,
withdrawal, suspicion, coldness, or control.

That is why Exodus 34:6 matters so deeply here.

The Father did not merely announce abstract attributes.
He revealed the shape of His own nature.

And right in the middle of that revelation is this overflowing
quality—**abundant in goodness**.
This is not a reluctant goodness.
This is not measured-out kindness with a calculator in hand.
This is love that leans toward blessing.

Loving-kindness is love leaning toward blessing.

Not because people earned it.
Not because the moment is convenient.
Not because the soul feels generous.

But because resurrection life has begun to rise higher than reaction.

That is the shift.

Before resurrection life matures in a believer, the soul asks:
What do I feel like doing?
What do they deserve?
How much do I have left?

But when the life of Christ begins to rise within, another question starts to lead:
What would love do here?

That is loving-kindness.

It is not weakness.
It is strength under government.
It is not passivity.
It is power choosing a better outcome.
It is not mere politeness.
It is the visible nature of God becoming tangible through a human life.

And that is why Scripture says His loving-kindness is *better than life.*

Because without loving-kindness, life may continue biologically...
but it does not feel like heaven.

2. JESUS DID NOT ONLY PREACH LOVE — HE CARRIED IT INTO PEOPLE

If you want to know what loving-kindness looks like, do not start with modern religious language.
Start with Jesus.

He was not soft because He was unsure.
He was gentle because He was governed.

He could speak to the wind.
He could rebuke demons.
He could overturn tables.
He could silence hypocrites.
But He could also stop for the ashamed, the overlooked, the unclean, the blind, the grieving, and the guilty.

That combination is important.

Because loving-kindness is not spineless sweetness.
It is holy strength that knows how to come near without losing truth.

Think of the woman taken in adultery.
The room was loaded with accusation.
Everyone had stones in their theology and murder in their hands.

Jesus did not join the mob.
He also did not call darkness light.

He disarmed the accusers.
He preserved the woman.
He restored the possibility of a new future.

That is loving-kindness.

Think of blind Bartimaeus crying out above the crowd.
Others wanted him quiet.
Jesus wanted him near.

Think of Jairus' house, full of fear and noise.
Jesus walked into panic with peace.

Think of Peter after the resurrection.
Peter had denied Him publicly.
Jesus did not restore him with humiliation.

He restored him with breakfast, questions, and recommissioning.

That is one of the most beautiful pictures in all of Scripture.

The firstborn from the dead did not come back breathing vengeance.
He came back carrying breakfast.

That is not a throwaway detail.
That is resurrection with personality.
That is the nature of God after the grave.

Loving-kindness is not the absence of holiness.
It is holiness expressed in a way that can still call people forward.

Jesus never lowered the standard.
He removed the fog around it.
He made righteousness feel like invitation, not just threat.

That is why sinners came near Him.

Not because He approved of sin.
But because they could feel that truth in Him was still somehow safe.

That is loving-kindness in full color.

3. LOVING-KINDNESS IS NOT TOLERANCE — IT IS REDEMPTIVE STRENGTH

This is an important distinction in our time.

The word **tolerance** gets thrown around as if it were the highest form of love.

But tolerance, as it is often used, simply means:
I will avoid conflict by refusing to deal with what is real.

That is not biblical loving-kindness.

Biblical loving-kindness does not avoid truth.
It carries truth in a way that still leaves room for
redemption.

Tolerance often abandons people in confusion so nobody
feels uncomfortable.
Loving-kindness moves toward people with enough courage
to help them come into the light.

Tolerance can be passive.
Loving-kindness is active.

Tolerance says, *Stay as you are, and I will call it peace.*
Loving-kindness says, *I care enough to walk with you
toward what is good.*

Tolerance may keep the room calm for a moment.
Loving-kindness can change a life.

That is why loving-kindness must never be confused with
cowardice.

When Jesus met the woman at the well, He did not flatter
her brokenness.
He exposed it without crushing her.
He revealed truth without making her unrecoverable.
And in doing so, He turned a wounded, isolated woman into
a witness.

That is not tolerance.
That is transformation wrapped in kindness.

This matters deeply for the reader.

Because some of us think we are being loving when we are actually avoiding discomfort.
And others think we are being truthful when we are actually just being sharp.

But the life in Christ is neither avoidance nor aggression.

It is truth carried in love.
It is love carrying truth.
It is the kind of presence where people can feel both the nearness of mercy and the weight of reality at the same time.

That is rare.
But it is exactly what resurrection life produces.

When God's life rises in you, you stop needing to win every moment.
You stop needing to protect your ego with hardness.
You stop needing to call passivity peace.

Instead, you begin to stand in the middle place—
firm enough to tell the truth,
warm enough to stay present,
clean enough to not manipulate,
steady enough to not run.

That is loving-kindness.

And the world is starving for it.

4. RESURRECTION LIFE MAKES LOVING-KINDNESS SUSTAINABLE

Anyone can be kind for five minutes.

Anyone can be warm when life is going their way.
Anyone can be generous when their soul is full, their

schedule is clear, and nobody is annoying them before breakfast.

But loving-kindness in Scripture is not mood-based.
It is nature-based.

This is why Chapter 5 matters so much.

If resurrection from the dead is reduced to only a future doctrine, then loving-kindness becomes an impossible standard people fake for short bursts.

But if resurrection from the dead includes the present rising of Christ's life in the believer, then loving-kindness becomes not merely a command...
but a fruit of shared life.

That is the difference between striving and abiding.

You can try to act nicer.
You can rehearse better words.
You can learn to smile through clenched teeth like a church greeter on fumes.

But eventually the soul runs out.

The Father is after something deeper.

He is not merely trying to improve your manners.
He is raising His Son's life in you.

That is why Paul says in Ephesians that God, who is rich in mercy, loved us, quickened us, and **raised us up together**.

Notice the sequence.

Mercy.
Love.
Raising.

The resurrection life of Christ is not disconnected from the nature of God.
It is the manifestation of it.

And when that life rises in you, loving-kindness becomes less theatrical and more natural.

You begin to pause before reacting.
You begin to see the wound under the behavior.
You begin to choose words that heal without lying.
You begin to stay in the room a little longer.
You begin to stop making every conflict about your own discomfort.
You begin to recognize that some people do not need your lecture first.
They need your steadiness.

This does not mean you become endlessly permissive.
It does not mean you never confront.
It does not mean you let chaos run the house.

It means the spirit is waking up.

And when the spirit is awake, the soul stops driving like a panic-stricken apprentice in the rain.

Loving-kindness is what it looks like when the life of Christ has enough room in you to touch others without your soul hijacking the job.

That is resurrection life becoming visible.

5. WHERE LOVING-KINDNESS IS SHOWING UP IN YOU

This is where the section becomes personal.

Because most readers do not struggle with the idea of loving-kindness.
They struggle with its timing.

They can see it in theory.
They can admire it in Jesus.
They can quote it in church.

But where does it go when:

- you are tired,
- interrupted,
- misunderstood,
- disappointed,
- under pressure,
- dealing with the same person again,
- or facing someone who clearly made the mess themselves?

That is where loving-kindness is tested.
And that is where resurrection life becomes visible.

Loving-kindness does not usually appear first in grand ministry moments.
It appears in ordinary frictions.

A delayed response.
A rude tone.
A family tension.
A repeated failure.
A person who drains you.
A conversation you did not want to have.
A wound that still knows your name.

This is where the believer begins to see whether the life of Christ is actually rising...
or whether the soul is still running the old script.

If your first instinct is always to withdraw, lash out, punish, harden, or silently keep score, that does not mean you are disqualified.

It means you have found the next place resurrection is needed.

That is a much gentler way to say it—
and a much truer one.

The point is not condemnation.
The point is recognition.

Because once you can see the pattern, you can bring it into the light.

And once it is in the light, it no longer has to keep ruling from the shadows.

This is one of the hidden mercies of God.

He often lets the same type of pressure return not merely because life is repetitive,
but because He is exposing the place where His nature is still trying to rise in you.

Not to shame you.
To free you.

So if you keep meeting the same kind of person...
or the same kind of trigger...
or the same kind of emotional collision...

do not only ask, *Why does this keep happening to me?*

Sometimes the better question is:
What quality of Christ is trying to come alive in me here?

In this section, the answer may well be:
loving-kindness.

6. REINFORCEMENT — LOVING-KINDNESS DOES NOT NEED TO BE FORCE-GROWN

Loving-kindness is not mere niceness.
It is not weakness.
It is not tolerance.
And it is not something the believer is meant to force-grow through pressure, performance, or religious strain.

Loving-kindness is the visible fruit of mercy, compassion, patience... and peace working together under the grace of God.

It does not need to be manufactured.
It needs to be matured.

That matters deeply.

Because many believers, once they see the beauty of Christ, immediately turn it into another burden for the soul to perform.

They see mercy and try to imitate it.
They see compassion and try to maintain it.
They see patience and try not to snap.
They see loving-kindness and think, *I need to become more like that by effort alone.*

But the life **In Christ** is not built by white-knuckled imitation.

It is grown by abiding.

Loving-kindness is not the fruit of panic.
It is the fruit of presence.

It is what begins to appear when mercy has had time to
soften you,
when compassion has had time to open you,
when patience has had time to steady you,
and when peace has had time to quiet the soul enough for
the life of Christ to come through.

That is why it often comes in season.

Not always all at once.
Not always instantly.
But truly.

And when it comes, it is no longer theatrical.
It is no longer borrowed language.
It is no longer spiritual posing.

It becomes part of your nature.

This is where grace must be heard clearly.

Christ did not come into the world to condemn the world,
but that through Him the world might be saved.

That means the movement of God toward us is not first
accusation, but rescue.
Not first exposure to destroy, but light to set free.

So when this section reveals places where loving-kindness is
still immature in you, the goal is not condemnation.

The goal is recognition under grace.

The Father is not standing over you demanding instant fruit.
He is growing His own nature in you.

And sometimes, like Paul with the thorn, we ask God to
remove the pressure...
while God is teaching us that His grace is already sufficient
within it.

Not because pain is the goal.
Not because struggle is holy in itself.
But because sometimes the deeper miracle is not immediate escape.

Sometimes the deeper miracle is that Christ becomes visible **in the middle of what used to rule you**.

That is resurrection life.

That is why loving-kindness is so precious.

It is not just that you were nice when you could have been harsh.
It is that something in you stayed steady where the old you would have reacted.

That is not personality polish.
That is evidence.

And this is where faith becomes beautifully practical.

Faith is a confident expectation that God will meet you in all areas of life.

So you do not have to panic when the fruit is still growing.
You do not have to fake maturity you do not yet carry.
You do not have to force what heaven intends to form.

You stay yielded.
You stay honest.
You stay near.
You keep walking **In Christ**.

And in season, loving-kindness will be there.

Not because you managed to manufacture it...
but because the life of Jesus kept rising in you.

If mercy, compassion, patience, and peace are the inner movements of resurrection life,
then loving-kindness is the first clear expression others can actually feel.

And from here, the final movement of the chapter comes into focus:

Because once love becomes visible, it must also become dependable.

That leads us straight into the last great triad:

Truth. Forgiveness. Justice.

Because the love of God is not only beautiful when it appears.
It is trustworthy when it remains.

GUIDED DISCOVERY — THE KINDNESS THAT STILL HAS BACKBONE

1. Where does your loving-kindness disappear first —at home, under pressure, in disappointment, or when someone repeats the same mistake?
Often the first place loving-kindness disappears is the place where the soul feels most entitled to react. That is not failure —it is revelation. It shows you where Christ's life is still asking for room.

2. Have you ever confused avoidance with peace, or sharpness with truth?
Many believers swing between silence and force. But Jesus carried neither passivity nor harshness. He carried truth in love. If you recognize either extreme in yourself, you are not discovering shame—you are discovering the doorway to maturity.

3. Can people feel safe around your truth, or only corrected by it?
Jesus could expose what was real without making people feel erased. That is a holy standard. If your truth leaves no room for restoration, it may still be carrying more soul than Spirit.

4. Are you waiting until you "feel loving" before you act like love?
Feelings matter, but loving-kindness is not sustained by mood. It is sustained by nature. As resurrection life rises in you, love becomes less dependent on your emotional weather and more dependent on who is alive within you.

5. What recurring relationship or pressure point may actually be revealing the next place resurrection needs to rise?
The repeated friction in your life may not only be an annoyance. It may be an invitation. God often exposes the same kind of tension until His nature becomes stronger there than your old reaction.

SECTION 5 — TRUTH, FORGIVENESS, AND JUSTICE

When the Love of God Becomes Dependable

Core Scripture

Exodus 34:6–7 (KJV) —
"The Lord, The Lord God, merciful and gracious, longsuffering, and abundant in goodness and

truth,
Keeping mercy for thousands, forgiving iniquity and transgression and sin, and that will by no means clear the guilty..."

Section Anchor Scriptures

John 1:14 (KJV) —
"And the Word was made flesh, and dwelt among us... full of grace and truth."

John 5:30 (KJV) —
"I can of mine own self do nothing... and my judgment is just; because I seek not mine own will, but the will of the Father which hath sent me."

John 8:11 (KJV) —
"...Neither do I condemn thee: go, and sin no more."

Psalm 89:14 (KJV) —
"Justice and judgment are the habitation of thy throne: mercy and truth shall go before thy face."

There comes a point in the journey where love must become more than a feeling.
More than a moment.
More than a tender impulse in the right environment.

If love is only present when the atmosphere is easy, it has not yet matured.
If it disappears the moment it is tested, it has not yet become dependable.

That is why Exodus 34 does not end with mercy, compassion, patience, and loving-kindness.
It moves deeper still.

It moves into **truth**.
It moves into **forgiveness**.
It moves into **justice**.

Because the love of God is not merely beautiful.
It is **stable**.

It is not only warm.
It is **trustworthy**.

It is not only comforting.
It is **safe to build a life on**.

This is where resurrection life becomes unmistakable.

A believer may speak kindly for a while.
A believer may be patient for a season.
A believer may even appear gentle when the cost is low.

But when truth must be spoken,
when forgiveness must be chosen,
when justice must be upheld,
that is where the real nature of the life within is revealed.

This final movement of Exodus 34 is not the softening of
love.
It is the **strengthening of love**.

Not love becoming harsher.
Love becoming **dependable**.

Because the world is full of people who have heard the
language of love while living under instability.
They have heard promises without follow-through.
Mercy without truth.
Forgiveness without change.
Correction without compassion.
Tolerance without transformation.
Judgment without righteousness.

But the Father is not fractured.
And Jesus did not reveal a divided God.

In Him, grace and truth are not enemies.
Mercy and justice do not fight.
Forgiveness and accountability do not cancel one another
out.

They live together perfectly in the nature of God.

And if resurrection from the dead means anything in the
believer now,
it means the nature of God is not only admired from a
distance.
It begins to rise into form **within us**.

**Resurrection life is not merely emotional warmth.
It is the dependable nature of God becoming visible
in the believer.**

1. Truth Is What Love Refuses to Betray

Truth is not merely factual accuracy.
It is not just correct information.
It is not simply being right in an argument.

In Scripture, truth is what can be **trusted**.
What holds.
What remains.
What does not shift when pressure comes.

Truth is what you can build on.

Without truth, mercy becomes sentiment.
Without truth, compassion becomes confusion.
Without truth, patience becomes passivity.
Without truth, loving-kindness becomes people-pleasing.

Truth is what gives love a backbone.

This is why Jesus is described as *full of grace and truth*.
Not grace without truth.
Not truth without grace.
Both.
Perfectly joined.

He did not flatter the rich young ruler.
He loved him enough to expose what owned him.

He did not condemn the woman caught in adultery.
He also did not rename her bondage as freedom.

He did not shame Peter after failure.
He restored him with piercing honesty.

Jesus never used truth as a weapon to dominate.
And He never used grace as an excuse to avoid truth.

That is resurrection life in motion.

Many people think truth is harsh because they have mostly
encountered it through the soul.
The soul uses truth to win.
To defend.
To prove.
To elevate self.
To expose others while hiding its own fear.

But truth in Christ does not come from ego.
It comes from love.

It does not arrive to humiliate.
It arrives to **set free**.

Christ did not come into the world to condemn the world,
but that through Him the world might be saved.

Truth is not the enemy of mercy.
Truth is mercy refusing to lie.

Truth is love refusing to cooperate with illusion.

Truth is the point where God's goodness becomes solid under your feet.

And this matters for the believer because resurrection life is not proven by how inspired we sound when everything is flowing.

It is proven by whether we are becoming dependable.

Can people trust our word?
Can they trust our spirit?
Can they trust our boundaries?
Can they trust our correction?
Can they trust that what we say in peace will still be true under pressure?

That is not perfection.
That is formation.

Because when the life of Christ matures in a man or woman, truth is no longer used to win arguments.
It becomes the ground others can stand on.

Truth is what makes love safe to trust.

2. Forgiveness Clears the Loop

Forgiveness is often misunderstood because people hear it through pain instead of through resurrection.

To the wounded soul, forgiveness can sound like weakness.
Like excusing evil.
Like pretending something did not matter.
Like giving permission for harm to continue.

But biblical forgiveness is none of those things.

Forgiveness is not denial.
It is not agreement with evil.
It is not the removal of consequence.
It is not the erasing of wisdom.
It is not the surrender of boundaries.

Forgiveness is **love releasing the debt it no longer needs to carry**.

And deeper still:

Forgiveness clears the looping condemnation so God's resurrection grace can flood the heart.

That line matters because many believers are not only carrying wounds from others.
They are also carrying accusations within themselves.

Old failures.
Old shame.
Old regrets.
Old replayed scenes.
Old inner verdicts.

The soul can become a courtroom that never adjourns.

It replays the case.
Rehearses the evidence.
Reissues the sentence.
And somehow still calls that discernment.

But condemnation is not discernment.
And looping accusation is not holiness.

If mercy opens the door,
if compassion moves toward pain,
if patience gives time,
if loving-kindness becomes visible,

forgiveness is where love refuses to become poisoned by what it has suffered,
and refuses to let shame keep ruling what grace is trying to raise.

Before long, the soul is keeping accounts.
Replaying conversations.
Building private courtrooms.
Preparing speeches no one asked for.
Living with invisible weight.

But resurrection life does not live by spiritual bookkeeping.

Because Christ has already shown us the pattern.

From the cross, while injustice was still active, He said,
"Father, forgive them; for they know not what they do."

That is not passivity.
That is not weakness.
That is the strength of divine life refusing to be redefined by the wound.

And Paul learned something similar in another place of pressure.

He asked for the thorn to be removed.
But the Lord answered him differently.

"My grace is sufficient for thee: for my strength is made perfect in weakness."

Sometimes we ask God to remove the pressure.
And sometimes He reveals that grace has already entered the place we thought was unbearable.

Not because pain is good.
But because resurrection life is stronger.

That is where forgiveness becomes possible.

Not because the event was small.
Not because the hurt was imaginary.
Not because trust is instantly restored.

But because the life of Christ in you is no longer willing to
let the wound become your master.

Forgiveness does not always mean immediate
reconciliation.
It does not always mean restored access.
It does not always mean the relationship returns to what it
was.

Sometimes forgiveness says,
"I release the debt before God,
but wisdom still guards the gate."

That is not contradiction.
That is maturity.

Because forgiveness without truth becomes foolish.
And forgiveness without justice becomes enabling.

But forgiveness in Christ is clean.

It releases what bitterness wants to keep alive.
It removes poison from the vessel.
It clears the looping condemnation.
And it makes room for resurrection grace to flood the heart
again.

That is resurrection.

Not merely surviving what happened.
Not merely coping.
But refusing to let death stay in the bloodstream.

**Forgiveness is resurrection life refusing to carry
what Christ already carried.**

3. Justice Is Love That Knows How to Judge

Justice is often feared because many have only known its counterfeit.

They have seen harshness called justice.
Control called justice.
Religious pride called justice.
Human revenge wrapped in holy language.

But biblical justice is not the anger of wounded ego wearing a robe.

Justice is **love defending what is good**.

Justice protects what mercy opened.
Justice guards what compassion moved toward.
Justice preserves what patience gave time to heal.
Justice keeps loving-kindness from becoming soft indulgence.
Justice keeps truth from being ignored.
Justice keeps forgiveness from being manipulated.

This is why Exodus 34 does not stop at mercy and forgiveness.
It says God forgives iniquity, transgression, and sin,
and **will by no means clear the guilty**.

Not because God is cruel.
Because He is trustworthy.

If evil had no answer, love would not be safe.
If corruption had no consequence, mercy would be mockery.
If oppression could endlessly continue without reckoning, compassion would have no teeth.

Justice is what tells the suffering,
"What happened matters."

Justice is what tells evil,
"You do not get the final word."

Justice is what tells creation,
"God's love is not weak."

And here Jesus becomes our clearest chart.

In **John 5:30**, He openly confessed His own inability:

"I can of mine own self do nothing…"

That is not weakness.
That is alignment.

He did not deny judgment.
He denied self-origin.

Then He immediately revealed the source of true judgment:

*"…and my judgment is just; because I seek not mine own
will, but the will of the Father which hath sent me."*

There it is.

Jesus confessed His inability,
but reinforced the Father's ability flowing through Him.

That is the pattern.

Judgment that rises from self is unstable.
Judgment that flows from the Father is true.

This is why:

**Judgment is not condemnation when it is flowing In
Christ.**

That line must be felt deeply.

Because condemnation comes from separation.
Judgment in Christ comes from alignment.

Condemnation seeks to crush.
Judgment seeks to reveal.

Condemnation pins identity to failure.
Judgment separates what is false so life can remain.

Condemnation says, "You are the darkness."
Judgment says, "This darkness cannot remain."

That is why Jesus could say to the woman caught in adultery:

"Neither do I condemn thee: go, and sin no more."

No condemnation.
Clear judgment.

No rejection.
Clear direction.

No shaming.
No pretending.

That is the flow of the Father.

And this is where many believers get confused.

Some think maturity means becoming endlessly tolerant.
Never confronting.
Never naming darkness.
Never drawing a line.
Never protecting what is vulnerable.

But tolerance is not the highest form of love.

Transformation is.

Love can be patient.
Love can be merciful.
Love can forgive.

And when necessary, love can still say:

"No further."

That is not flesh.
That is not ego.
That is not legalism.

That is the nature of God becoming dependable in a human life.

And this is the final station stop before Eternal Judgment for a reason.

Because before Scripture speaks of the final accounting, it teaches us the nature of the One who judges.

He is not random.
He is not unstable.
He is not vindictive.

He is merciful.
Compassionate.
Patient.
Abundant in loving-kindness.
Full of truth.
Rich in forgiveness.
And unwavering in justice.

That is not contradiction.
That is glory.

Justice is not love becoming cruel.
Justice is love refusing to abandon what is good.

4. The Captain Now Has His Charts

By now the reader should feel it.

Chapter 5 has not merely been about a future event called resurrection.
It has been about a present unveiling.

Yes, there is a resurrection to come.
Yes, there is a catching up for those who are truly **In Christ**.
Yes, death itself will finally bow.

But long before that day, resurrection is meant to become a pattern in the life of the believer now.

Not simply a doctrine we defend.
A nature we embody.

And that nature has now been shown in full through Exodus 34:

Mercy.
Compassion.
Patience.
Loving-kindness.
Truth.
Forgiveness.
Justice.

This is not merely a list of attributes.
It is a portrait of the Father.

It is the grain of divine love.

It is the life Jesus revealed perfectly.

And it is the life the Spirit is pressing toward in those who abide **In Christ**.

This is why this chapter matters so much.

Because many have been taught to think of resurrection only as escape.

Escape from the earth.
Escape from suffering.
Escape from death.
Escape from judgment.

But resurrection is more than escape.

It is **God's life rising in the believer until His nature becomes visible**.

That is the deeper witness.

And if that life is truly rising, then something begins to change.

You stop needing to be right all the time, because truth is becoming deeper than ego.
You stop needing to collect debts, because forgiveness is becoming stronger than pain.
You stop confusing passivity with peace, because justice is teaching you how to protect what is good.
You stop performing kindness for appearance, because loving-kindness is maturing naturally in season.
You stop forcing fruit, because you begin to trust the root.

Loving-kindness is a fruit.
It does not need to be force-grown.
It matures where mercy, compassion, and patience have truly taken root.

And this is where faith quietly becomes vital again.

Not faith as religious strain.
Not faith as mental squeezing.
Not faith as pretending harder.

But faith as **confident expectation that God will meet you in every area of life**.

Because if resurrection life is truly His life in you,
then you are not being asked to manufacture divine nature.

You are being invited to yield to it.

The soul tries to perform holiness.
The Spirit forms Christ.

The soul imitates.
The Spirit grows.

The soul strains to look alive.
The Spirit raises the dead.

And now, at the close of this section, the captain has his charts.

Not because every wave is gone.
Not because every storm has passed.
Not because the sea has become flat.

But because the nature of the Father has been revealed in a way the soul can no longer honestly ignore.

The course is now visible.

Mercy.
Compassion.
Patience.
Loving-kindness.
Truth.
Forgiveness.
Justice.

This is the chart of resurrection life.

This is what it looks like when the risen Christ is not only believed in,
but trusted enough to be formed within.

The captain now has his charts to navigate by.

Guided Discovery

1. Do I confuse being loving with avoiding truth?
If truth only appears in your life when frustration leaks out,
then truth is probably still being carried by the soul instead
of by love.
But if Christ is forming in you, truth becomes clean, calm,
and freeing.
It does not arrive to win.
It arrives to heal what lies have held in place.

**2. Am I still carrying loops that forgiveness was
meant to clear?**
Some burdens feel spiritual when they are actually
accumulated pain, shame, or old accusation.
If you are replaying old wounds, rehearsing old speeches, or
reliving old failures, the soul may still be carrying what
Christ is inviting you to release.
Forgiveness does not erase wisdom, but it does clear the
looping condemnation so grace can flood the heart again.

**3. Have I mistaken condemnation for judgment, or
passivity for peace?**
Condemnation crushes identity.
Judgment in Christ reveals what must go so life can remain.
And peace is not the absence of confrontation.
Sometimes peace requires a boundary.
Sometimes peace requires a clear word.
Sometimes peace requires protecting what is good before
further damage is done.

Resurrection life is not only the promise that we will rise one day.
It is the proof that God's love can become dependable in us now.

The Final Station Stop Before Eternal Judgment

Resurrection from the dead is not only the promise that life continues after the grave.
It is the unveiling of what kind of life God is raising in His people even now.

If this chapter has done its work, then the reader should no longer hear resurrection as a distant trumpet only.
They should hear it as a present invitation.

An invitation to stop treating salvation as mere rescue language.
An invitation to stop resting in symbols while avoiding transformation.
An invitation to let the life of Christ rise past vocabulary and into visible nature.

Because the Father has now been shown.

Not as abstraction.
Not as doctrine alone.
But as revealed nature:

Mercy.
Compassion.
Patience.
Loving-kindness.
Truth.
Forgiveness.
Justice.

This is the life of the risen Christ.
This is the pattern of the new creation.
This is what resurrection is pressing toward in those who
are truly **In Christ**.

This chapter has not been asking the reader merely,
"Do you believe that the dead will rise?"

It has been asking something deeper.

Do you recognize the kind of life God is raising in you now?

Because resurrection is not only about the body one day.
It is about the nature of Christ taking form in the believer
now.

Not merely a future event.
A present formation.

Not merely something to wait for.
Something to yield to.

That is why this chapter had to move the way it did.

It began by clearing the common misunderstanding that
resurrection belongs only to the end.
It turned the reader's face toward Jesus, the Firstborn from
the dead—the only man in human history not merely
revived, but truly resurrected through death into a new
creation life.
It then walked through the revealed nature of God in
Exodus 34:6, not as a theological list, but as the living
pattern of resurrection life:

Mercy that chooses kindness from strength.
Compassion that moves toward suffering.
Patience that gives time for repentance and growth.
Loving-kindness that ripens as the visible fruit of love.
Truth that becomes dependable under pressure.

Forgiveness that releases what death tries to keep looping.
Justice that defends what is good.

This is not random progression.

It is a chart.

The captain now has his charts to navigate by.

Not because every wave is gone.
Not because every storm has passed.
But because the nature of the Father has now been revealed
in a way the soul can no longer honestly ignore.

The course is visible.

And that matters, because once the reader sees resurrection
rightly,
only one doctrine remains.

Eternal Judgment.

And for many, that phrase immediately tightens the chest.

Because they have heard it preached as threat.
As doom.
As religious leverage.
As fear without context.
As a final hammer in the hand of unstable men.

But that is not how it must be received.

Because before a reader can understand judgment rightly,
they must first trust the Judge.

And that is why Chapter 5 had to end here.

Before Scripture speaks of the final weighing of all things,
it first shows us the nature of the One who weighs them.

He is not cold.
He is not unstable.
He is not vindictive.
He is not arbitrary.
He is not eager to condemn.

He is merciful.
Compassionate.
Patient.
Abundant in loving-kindness.
Full of truth.
Rich in forgiveness.
And unwavering in justice.

That is not a contradiction.

That is the very reason judgment can be trusted.

Because judgment in Scripture is not meant to be
understood through the lens of human volatility.
It is meant to be understood through the revealed nature of
God.

And here Jesus becomes the bridge.

He said:

"I can of mine own self do nothing…"
**"…and my judgment is just; because I seek not
mine own will, but the will of the Father which
hath sent me."**
— John 5:30

There is the final key before the next chapter.

Jesus did not deny judgment.
He denied self-origin.

He openly confessed His own inability,
and immediately revealed the Father as the source of what is true.

That is the pattern.

Judgment that rises from self condemns.
Judgment that flows from the Father reveals.

Judgment that rises from ego crushes.
Judgment that flows **In Christ** separates darkness from life.

This is why we must say it plainly:

Judgment is not condemnation when it is flowing In Christ.

Condemnation pins identity to failure.
Judgment reveals what must be removed so life can remain.

Condemnation says,
"You are the darkness."

Judgment says,
"This darkness cannot remain."

Condemnation closes the door.
Judgment opens the way forward.

Condemnation is the soul weaponizing failure.
Judgment is love establishing what is true.

That is why Jesus could say to the woman caught in adultery:

"Neither do I condemn thee: go, and sin no more."

No condemnation.
Clear judgment.

No rejection.
Clear direction.

No shaming.
No pretending.

That is the flow of the Father.

And if that is true in the earthly ministry of Jesus,
then it becomes the only safe lens through which to enter
the final doctrine.

Because **Eternal Judgment** is not the contradiction of
everything we have just seen.

It is the **establishment** of it.

It is not the moment where love disappears and severity
takes over.

It is the moment where all things are finally weighed by
what is true.

Everything.

Every work.
Every motive.
Every hidden thing.
Every false support.
Every empty performance.
Every act of love.
Every yielded yes.
Every place where Christ was formed.
Every place where the soul resisted.
Every place where grace was received.
Every place where it was refused.

Nothing false will stand there.
Nothing hidden will remain hidden.
Nothing unstable will be able to pretend it was solid.

And yet even here, the reader must not lose the thread.

The One who weighs all things
is the very One who first loved them.

The One who sees clearly
is the very One who made mercy known.

The One who judges justly
is the same One who is full of grace and truth.

The One who exposes darkness
is the same One who calls the dead to rise.

That is why this chapter had to end before the reader ever
arrives at the final doctrine.

Because if they do not first see the Father in Christ,
they will misunderstand judgment.

They will hear threat where Scripture is revealing truth.
They will hear fear where Scripture is revealing order.
They will hear rejection where Scripture is revealing
separation.
They will hear distance where Scripture is revealing the final
triumph of what is real.

So let the final line of this chapter settle deeply before
moving on:

**Resurrection from the dead is not only the promise
that we will rise one day.
It is the proof that God's love can become
dependable in us now.**

And once that is seen,
the final doctrine can be received with steady hands.

Not as panic.
Not as pressure.
Not as the last weapon of religion.

But as the sober and holy revelation
that **everything is weighed by what is true**.

And that is the final station stop before the last chapter:

**the believer learning that the One who weighs all things
is the very One who first loved them.**

CHAPTER 6 — ETERNAL JUDGMENT

The Final Clarity of God's Love

Core Scripture:
Hebrews 6:1–2 (KJV) — *"Therefore leaving the principles of the doctrine of Christ, let us go on unto perfection... of the resurrection of the dead, and of eternal judgment."*

Primary Anchor:
John 5:30 (KJV) — *"I can of mine own self do nothing: as I hear, I judge: and my judgment is just; because I seek not mine own will, but the will of the Father which hath sent me."*

Secondary Anchors:
Romans 8:1 (KJV) — *"There is therefore now no condemnation to them which are in Christ Jesus..."*

1 John 4:18 (KJV) — *"There is no fear in love; but perfect love casteth out fear: because fear hath torment..."*

Revelation 3:21 (KJV) — *"To him that overcometh will I grant to sit with me in my throne, even as I also overcame..."*
Galatians 5:22–23 (KJV) — *"...against such there is no law."*

Eternal judgment is often spoken of in a way that makes the soul tense before the spirit can listen.
For many, the phrase has been wrapped in fear, urgency, and images so heavy that the heart hears threat before it hears truth.
But the doctrine of Christ does not end by pushing the reader back into terror.
It ends by bringing everything into the light.

This final doctrine must be handled with care, because what many people call "judgment" is often only the echo of Adam's first fear.

Ever since the fall, humanity has lived with an inward sense of exposure, shame, and compensation.

The soul learned to hide, to strive, to compare, to defend, and to cover itself.
It learned to expect that being seen would lead to pain.
This is why so many hear the word judgment and immediately feel condemnation.

But in Christ, something changes.
The same scriptures that speak of judgment also reveal something remarkable: ***"There is therefore now no condemnation to them which are in Christ Jesus."***

Not less truth.
Not less holiness.
Not less accountability.
But no condemnation.

This means that in Christ, judgment remains—but condemnation does not.

The believer is not being invited into denial.
He is being invited into rightly aligned judgment, where truth no longer drives him into hiding but draws him into freedom.

This is why **John 5:30** stands at the center of this chapter. Jesus does not speak of judgment as emotional reaction, sudden anger, or independent force.

He says, ***"As I hear, I judge: and my judgment is just..."***
His judgment is just because it is perfectly aligned with the Father.

It is not ego.
It is not insecurity.
It is not a knee-jerk reaction.
It is fixed wisdom flowing from perfect love.
It is the dependable separation of what is true from what is false, what is life from what is death, what can remain from what cannot.

This is why eternal judgment must not be understood as a divine temper. It is better understood as a divine safeguard.

Eternal judgment is the fixed wisdom of God that protects freedom, truth, and love forever.

It is the eternal safety rail of the Kingdom.
It does not destroy freedom; it makes freedom safe.
It does not cancel love; it protects what love is.
It does not remove choice; it reveals what each path produces.
God's judgments are not random punishments.

They are the settled wisdom of a perfect Father whose ways are trustworthy.

And this is where the final chapter of *The Doctrine of Christ* becomes deeply personal.
Because this is not only about the end of all things.
It is about the healing of humanity's first misjudgment.

Adam hid because he no longer trusted what being seen by God would mean.

Jesus came and revealed the Father.

The overcomer learns to stand where Adam fled.
He learns that perfect love casts out fear, because fear grows where judgment has been wrongly understood.
And as that fear is removed, the believer begins to see what eternal judgment truly is: not the final panic of the soul, but the final clarity of God.

This chapter is not written to frighten the reader into outward compliance.
It is written to bring the reader into deeper trust.

Because the Judge on the throne is the Lamb who was slain.
The One who judges is the One who first loved you.
The One who calls the overcomer is the One who overcame first.

The final doctrine of Christ is not meant to leave you trembling at the edge of rejection, but standing in the light of what remains forever **In Christ**.

CHAPTER 6 OVERVIEW — THE FIVE STATIONS OF ETERNAL JUDGMENT

1. WHY THE SOUL FEARS JUDGMENT

This first section meets the reader exactly where many already live: under the weight of fear, inner accusation, striving, and the dread of being exposed. It gently acknowledges the human experience of condemnation without minimizing it, helping the reader understand that these responses are deeply familiar—but they are not the final truth.

2. THE FIRST MISALIGNED JUDGMENT

This section traces the human story back to Adam, where fear, shame, hiding, blame, and self-protection first entered the soul. It reveals how condemnation became the atmosphere of fallen humanity and why so much striving is simply the soul trying to compensate for separation.

3. THE OVERCOMING THREAD

This section follows the common thread of those who learned to move toward God in trust rather than hide from Him in fear. From the faithful witnesses of old to Jesus Christ as the perfect and final Overcomer, it shows that overcoming is not about flawless performance, but about remaining aligned with truth, faith, and God's love.

4. JUDGMENT WITHOUT CONDEMNATION

Here the doctrine becomes clear and mature. This section separates true judgment from accusation and shows that in Christ, truth still stands while condemnation loses its voice.

It reveals that perfect love casts out fear because God's judgments are not unstable reactions, but the fixed wisdom that protects freedom, truth, and love forever.

5. THE FINAL SEPARATION AND THE INHERITANCE OF LOVE

The final section brings the chapter—and the book—to its strongest conclusion. It carefully explores what cannot remain, what is finally revealed, and what endures forever. With sober clarity and deep hope, it points to the overcomer, the Lamb's book of life, the city of God, and the eternal inheritance of those who remain **In Christ**.

Condemnation hides in the trees.
Perfect love calls us back into the light.

SECTION 1 — WHY THE SOUL FEARS JUDGMENT

Why even the mention of judgment can make the heart shrink—until love teaches it the difference.

Core Scripture:
Romans 8:1 (KJV) — *"There is therefore now no condemnation to them which are in Christ Jesus, who walk not after the flesh, but after the Spirit."*

1 John 4:18 (KJV) — *"There is no fear in love; but perfect love casteth out fear: because fear hath torment..."*

The moment many people hear the word **judgment**,
something inside them tightens.
Even sincere believers can feel it.
A quiet flinch.
A subtle heaviness.
A reflex to brace.
Not because they necessarily reject God...
but because the soul has been trained to associate judgment
with **condemnation, rejection, exposure, and pain**.

That reaction did not begin in church.
It began much deeper.
It lives in the human story itself.

For many, judgment feels like standing in the light while
expecting to be shamed.
It feels like being measured and found lacking.
It feels like the old inner courtroom where the soul has
already learned to prosecute itself before anyone else can.
And so when the subject appears, the soul does what it has
always done:
it hides, it strives, or it hardens.

But this is exactly why we must begin here.

Before we can understand **eternal judgment** as one of the
foundational doctrines of Christ, we must first separate
what the wounded soul feels...
from what the Father is actually like.

Because if judgment is approached through fear alone, it
will always be misread.
But if it is approached **In Christ**, through the lens of God's
love, something changes.

The same word that once felt threatening begins to become
stabilizing.

The thing that once sounded like danger begins to reveal itself as safety.

1. THE SOUL HEARS "JUDGMENT" AND EXPECTS CONDEMNATION

Most people do not fear the truth because truth is evil.
They fear what they think truth will cost them.

The soul remembers failure.
It remembers shame.
It remembers moments of exposure.
It remembers being misunderstood, blamed, rejected, or corrected without tenderness.
And over time, it begins to build a protective system around itself.

This is why many people do not merely avoid sin...
they avoid **being seen**.

They avoid prayer when they feel distant.
They avoid honest reflection when they feel weak.
They avoid deeper surrender when they suspect it may uncover something painful.
They may still speak the language of faith, attend church, quote scripture, and carry on outwardly...
but inwardly, part of the soul is still standing behind fig leaves.

That is why **Romans 8:1** is not a small verse.
It is a rescue line.

"There is therefore now no condemnation to them which are in Christ Jesus..."

Notice what Paul does not say.
He does not say there is no truth.
He does not say there is no correction.

He does not say there is no judgment.
He says there is **now no condemnation** to those **In Christ**.

That is a massive distinction.

Condemnation is not the same as judgment.
Condemnation crushes identity.
God's judgment reveals reality.
Condemnation says, *You are cast off.*
God's judgment says, *This is true, and this is the way of life.*
Condemnation pushes the soul into hiding.
God's love in Christ brings the soul into the light so it can heal.

The soul hears *judgment* and thinks, *I am in danger.*
But the Spirit begins to teach:

In Christ, truth is not arriving to destroy you.
It is arriving to free you.

2. FEAR, STRIVING, AND HIDING ARE OFTEN THE SAME ROOT IN DIFFERENT CLOTHES

When the soul is afraid of judgment, it rarely just sits still and announces itself.
It puts on costumes.

Sometimes it becomes **striving**.

A person begins to live as though acceptance must be earned.
They overcompensate.
They perform.
They exhaust themselves trying to stay ahead of their own inner accusation.

They become deeply familiar with spiritual effort...
but not always with spiritual rest.

Sometimes it becomes **hiding**.

A person pulls back from intimacy with God.
They stay near enough to feel religious, but not near enough
to be fully seen.
They keep conversations safe.
They keep prayers polished.
They avoid the places where love might touch what has been
buried.

Sometimes it becomes **hardness**.

The soul learns to pre-judge everything before it can be
judged.
It becomes critical.
Defensive.
Opinionated.
Quick to measure others.
Because if the inner world is unresolved, projecting outward
can feel safer than being searched within.

This is why fear of judgment is not just a doctrinal
misunderstanding.
It is often a **life pattern**.

And this is where **1 John 4:18** begins to speak softly but
powerfully:

*"There is no fear in love; but perfect love casteth out fear:
because fear hath torment..."*

John does not merely say fear is uncomfortable.
He says fear has **torment**.

That is exactly what condemnation feels like.
It loops.

It nags.
It accuses.
It predicts disaster.
It makes the soul rehearse old failures and future threats.
It keeps a person moving, but never resting.
Talking, but never opening.
Believing in God, but not always trusting His heart.

And then John says something revolutionary:
perfect love casts it out.

Not polished religion.
Not stronger self-effort.
Not better image management.
Not spiritual cosmetics over soul panic.

Perfect love.

Which means the answer to the fear of judgment is not the
removal of truth.
It is the revelation of the Father's heart **through truth**.

3. THE GOSPEL DOES NOT REMOVE JUDGMENT—IT REMOVES THE TORMENT OF MISREADING IT

This is where many believers quietly get stuck.

If we only preach, *"Don't worry, you're saved,"* but never
teach the soul how to live **In Christ**, the inner fear can
remain.
The language of salvation may be present...
while the reflex of condemnation still quietly governs the
heart.

A person can say, *"I believe in grace,"*
while still living as though one wrong move will make God
pull away.

A person can say, *"I know God loves me,"*
while still internally flinching every time the light gets close.
A person can speak about freedom,
yet still live under the hidden management system of shame.

This is why this chapter matters.

**Eternal judgment is not the doctrine of eternal
condemnation.**
It is not God flying off the handle.
It is not divine mood swings.
It is not heavenly irritation made permanent.

**Eternal judgment is the fixed wisdom of God that
protects freedom, truth, and love forever.**

That is why the soul must first be calmed before it can
receive the doctrine rightly.

If the soul still hears "judgment" as "I am doomed," it will
resist the very rails that were meant to protect life.
But once the soul begins to understand that God's
judgments are the dependable outflow of His nature…
then the doctrine changes shape in the reader's hands.

It no longer feels like a threat hanging over them.
It begins to feel like a foundation under them.

4. JESUS DID NOT COME TO LEAVE US IN FEAR—HE CAME TO BRING US INTO THE LIGHT WITHOUT CONDEMNATION

Jesus never handled broken people the way fear expected.

The guilty woman expected stones.
He gave truth, dignity, and a way forward.

The ashamed expected rejection.
He gave invitation.
The striving expected more burden.
He gave rest.
The hiding expected exposure unto humiliation.
He brought exposure unto healing.

This is why His presence matters so much in this chapter.

Jesus did not come to erase the Father's judgments.
He came to **reveal them properly**.

He showed that God's judgments are not detached legal
reactions.
They flow from the heart of the Father.
They are aligned with truth.
They are filled with purpose.
They protect what is real.
They expose what destroys.
They invite what is life-giving.
And when received **In Christ**, they do not crush the one
who comes honestly…
they begin to restore them.

This is why **Romans 8:1** and **1 John 4:18** belong together.

No condemnation.
No tormenting fear.
Not because truth vanished…
but because **God's love in Christ changed the way
truth reaches us.**

And that is where many readers need to breathe for a
moment.

Because some have spent years thinking their discomfort
around judgment was proof they were spiritually sensitive…
when in reality, it may simply be proof that the soul has not
yet learned the difference between **condemnation** and

correction, between **torment** and **truth**, between **fear** and **the safety of being fully known in love**.

GUIDED DISCOVERY — WHERE DOES YOUR SOUL GO WHEN TRUTH GETS CLOSE?

When the subject of judgment comes up, do you feel drawn toward God—or do you instinctively brace yourself?

If your first inner movement is tension, heaviness, or the urge to pull back, that does not automatically mean you are rebellious.
It may simply mean your soul has learned to associate exposure with pain.
That is exactly why the gospel is so precious.
God does not shame that reaction.
He gently retrains it.
In Christ, the light is no longer arriving to destroy you.
It is arriving to bring what is hidden into a place where love can heal it.

Do you find yourself striving to stay acceptable, as though peace with God must be maintained by constant performance?

If so, you may be feeling the weight of condemnation even while believing the words of grace.
Striving is often fear wearing a respectable suit.
It looks disciplined on the outside, but underneath it can be a soul trying to outrun accusation.
Romans 8:1 is not merely a comforting verse—it is an invitation to stop building fig leaves out of effort.
In Christ, acceptance is not something you are frantically trying to secure.
It is the place from which transformation begins.

When truth exposes something in you, do you hear invitation—or accusation?

This question matters deeply.
Because the same moment of exposure can feel completely different depending on which voice you are hearing.
Accusation says, *You are the problem. Hide.*
Love says, *This is the problem. Come closer.*
Accusation isolates.
Love restores.
Accusation drives you into torment.
Perfect love casts out fear because it teaches the soul that being seen by God is not the end of safety—it is the beginning of healing.

If any of these questions touched something tender in you, do not rush past it.
That tenderness may be the doorway.
Not the doorway into shame...
but the doorway into understanding why this doctrine has often been misheard.

The soul fears judgment when it does not yet know the heart behind it.
But once the heart of the Father is seen in Christ, the word begins to change.
The flinch begins to soften.
The hiding begins to lose its power.
And the soul becomes ready to ask a deeper question:

Where did this misalignment begin?

Because the fear did not appear out of nowhere.
There was a first fracture.
A first false conclusion.
A first moment where human judgment moved out of alignment with God's love.

And that is where we go next.

Before we can understand eternal judgment as the fixed wisdom of God, we must go back to the first moment human judgment bent out of shape.

Not at Sinai.
Not in church history.
Not in the law.

But in the garden.

The soul did not begin by fearing God's judgment.
It began by **misjudging God Himself**.

And once that happened, fear entered the human story.

SECTION 2 — THE FIRST MISALIGNED JUDGMENT

How the first wrong conclusion about God taught humanity to hide. The soul did not first fear punishment. It first feared what it believed God had become.

Core Scripture:
Genesis 3:8–10 (KJV) — *"And they heard the voice of the Lord God walking in the garden in the cool of the day: and Adam and his wife hid themselves from the presence of the Lord God amongst the trees of the garden. And the Lord God called unto Adam, and said unto him, Where art thou?*

And he said, I heard thy voice in the garden, and I was afraid, because I was naked; and I hid myself."

From the beginning, the issue was not simply sin.
It was what sin produced in the soul when truth became distorted.

Adam and Eve did not only break trust.
They immediately formed a conclusion.

A judgment.
A misaligned one.

They did not run because God had changed.
They ran because their perception of Him had changed.

And that one shift has echoed through humanity ever since.

The moment love was questioned, fear entered.
The moment fear entered, hiding began.
The moment hiding began, striving followed close behind.

This is why so much of the human story is not simply rebellion.
It is reaction.

It is the soul trying to manage the pain of separation while drawing conclusions about God it was never meant to carry.

And if we are going to understand eternal judgment rightly, we must first understand this:

The first judgment that damaged humanity was not God's judgment of man.
It was man's false judgment of God.

1. The First Inner Verdict Was Formed in Fear

When Adam said, *"I was afraid... and I hid myself,"* he revealed more than emotion.
He revealed interpretation.

Fear had already reached a conclusion.

Something in the soul had shifted from:
"God is my covering"
to
"God is now unsafe."

That is the first misaligned judgment.

Notice carefully—God had not yet thundered from heaven.
He had not yet cast them from the garden.
He had not yet spoken the consequences.

Yet Adam was already hiding.

Why?

Because the soul had already judged the situation.
And more importantly, it had judged **God** through the lens of shame.

This is still how the soul works now.

When shame rises, the soul often does not wait for truth.
It reaches for a conclusion.

It assumes rejection.
It anticipates exposure.
It predicts distance.
It braces for punishment.
It starts writing a story before the Father has even spoken.

And once that story is written, hiding feels wise.

That is why so many people live as though God is angry first
and loving second.
They have inherited Adam's panic without realizing it.

They do not always say it out loud.
But deep inside, the soul whispers:

- "I have failed, so He must be pulling away."
- "I feel exposed, so I must no longer be safe."
- "I made the wrong choice, so now I must manage this alone."
- "If I come close, I may be condemned."

That is not the voice of the Father.
That is the echo of the garden through an unhealed soul.

**Fear often feels like wisdom to the wounded soul.
But fear is a terrible theologian.**

2. The Enemy Did Not Need to Remove God's Love—Only to Distort It

The serpent's strategy in the garden was subtle.

He did not begin by saying, *"God hates you."*
He began by planting suspicion.

"Yea, hath God said...?"
(Genesis 3:1, KJV)

That is where the fracture begins.

Not with open rebellion first.
With mistrust.

Not with visible collapse first.
With an inward reinterpretation.

The enemy did not need Adam and Eve to stop believing
God existed.
He only needed them to question whether God was fully
good.

That is still the ancient strategy.

If the enemy can bend the image of the Father in the mind
of the soul, then fear will do the rest.

Once love is doubted, the soul becomes unstable.
Once the soul becomes unstable, it reaches for self-
protection.
Once self-protection takes over, hiding, blame, control,
performance, and striving all begin to feel normal.

That is exactly what happened in the garden.

They hid.
They covered themselves.
They blamed each other.
They shifted responsibility.
They moved out of relational openness into defensive
survival.

All of it flowed from one poisoned conclusion:

"I can no longer trust how God sees me."

That is devastating.
Because the very One they needed most in that moment was
the One they now feared.

And this is why so many believers can sincerely love Jesus,
yet still live emotionally distant from the Father.

They may confess truth with their lips, yet still react to God through the old nervous system of Adam.

They know the verses.
But when failure comes, they still hide.
When weakness shows, they still brace.
When conviction comes, they confuse it with rejection.

Yet conviction is not rejection.
Light is not cruelty.
Truth is not abandonment.

**The enemy's first victory was not making man sin.
It was making man misread God after sin.**

3. God's First Response Was Not Distance—It Was Pursuit

This is one of the most beautiful moments in all of Scripture.

After the fall...
God comes walking.

Not because He did not know what happened.
Not because He was confused.
Not because heaven had lost track of Adam.

He comes because love still moves toward the hiding place.

"And the Lord God called unto Adam, and said unto him, Where art thou?"
(Genesis 3:9, KJV)

This is not the cry of a tyrant hunting prey.
This is the voice of a Father drawing out a son.

"Where art thou?"

Not, *"Why are you worthless?"*
Not, *"How dare you show your face?"*
Not, *"Stay hidden until you fix yourself."*

Even in the moment of disobedience, the movement of God is still relational.

He comes near.
He calls out.
He invites truth into the open.

This is crucial for the reader to feel.

The first divine movement after man's failure was not abandonment.
It was pursuit.

Yes, consequences would follow.
Yes, truth would be spoken.
Yes, the garden would change.

But before any of that is fully unfolded, we are shown something foundational:

God does not stop moving toward people when they fail.

That single revelation begins to dismantle the soul's ancient lie.

The soul says, "Hide until you are safe."
The Father says, "Come out, because I am here."

The soul says, "Cover yourself before He sees."
The Father says, "I already see, and I am still speaking."

The soul says, "Distance will protect me."
The Father says, "Only truth in My presence will heal you."

This is the beginning of restoring judgment.

Because right judgment begins when we stop interpreting
God through shame and start interpreting ourselves through
His love.

4. Humanity Has Been Repeating the Garden Ever Since

The garden was not merely an event.
It became a pattern.

Adam hid behind trees.
Humanity has been hiding behind everything else ever
since.

Some hide behind religion.
Some hide behind performance.
Some hide behind knowledge.
Some hide behind busyness.
Some hide behind humor.
Some hide behind ministry.
Some hide behind strength.
Some hide behind silence.
Some hide behind control.

But the root is often the same:

**"If I am fully seen in this condition, I may not be
safe."**

That is the old misaligned judgment still working in the
soul.

This is why condemnation is so powerful.
It does not merely accuse behavior.
It distorts relationship.

It does not simply say, *"You did wrong."*
It quietly adds, *"And now God must be different toward
you."*

That is the poison.

But Romans 8:1 cuts directly across that inherited lie:

**"There is therefore now no condemnation to them
which are in Christ Jesus…"**
(Romans 8:1, KJV)

That does not mean truth disappears.
It means the relationship is no longer governed by
condemnation.

It means that in Christ, the old Adamic reflex is being
undone.

The soul may still try to hide.
But the Spirit now teaches us another way.

The soul may still brace.
But grace teaches us to come near.

The soul may still predict rejection.
But the cross reveals the Father has already moved toward
us in His Son.

This is why so much of spiritual growth is not merely
learning more doctrine.
It is allowing the misjudgments of the soul to be corrected
by the revealed nature of God.

And what is that nature?

Mercy.
Compassion.
Patience.
Loving-kindness.

Truth.
Forgiveness.
Justice.

The same God Adam feared in distortion is the God fully revealed in Jesus Christ.

Jesus is not the nicer version of the Father.
Jesus is the clear revelation of the Father Adam misjudged.

That line matters deeply here.

Because the chapter is not just trying to explain judgment.
It is trying to heal the reader's interpretation of God.

5. The Healing Begins When We Revisit the Garden Through Christ

Most people read Genesis 3 as the story of man's failure.
And it is.

But it is also the story of man's first false conclusion about God.

And until that false conclusion is healed, the soul will keep reacting as though love has conditions it does not have.

This is why 1 John later says:

"There is no fear in love; but perfect love casteth out fear: because fear hath torment. He that feareth is not made perfect in love."
1 John 4:18 (KJV)

John is not describing shallow emotion.
He is describing restored judgment.

Fear has torment because fear is always anticipating something.
It is predicting harm.
It is bracing for loss.
It is expecting rejection, punishment, or abandonment.

In other words, fear is a form of judgment in the soul.

It is the soul saying:
"I know what this means, and it is not good."

But perfect love casts that out. Why? Because perfect love realigns the conclusion.

Perfect love teaches the soul:

- God has not changed because you are exposed.
- Truth is not the enemy of intimacy.
- Conviction is not condemnation.
- Being seen is not the same as being rejected.
- The Father's nearness is not removed by your weakness.
- In Christ, you are being taught to stop hiding.

This is where eternal judgment begins to feel different.

Not as a looming threat over fragile people.
But as the dependable wisdom of God that protects freedom, truth, and love forever.

And before we can stand in that wisdom, the first lie must be broken.

The first lie was not only that man could be like God without God.
The first lie was also that once man fell, God could no longer be trusted.

Jesus answers both.

Guided Discovery — Let the Garden Speak Honestly

1. When you fail, what is your first inward instinct—move toward God, or manage yourself first?
If your first reflex is to hide, fix yourself, numb out, perform, or withdraw, you are not unusual—you are feeling the old garden reflex in the soul. But that reflex is not your final truth. In Christ, you are being retrained to come into the light instead of running from it.

2. Have you ever mistaken conviction for rejection?
Many people have. Conviction says, *"This needs healing."* Condemnation says, *"You are no longer safe."* The Father corrects because He loves. The accuser condemns because he wants distance. Learning the difference is one of the great turning points in spiritual maturity.

3. What if God's first movement toward your weakness is still pursuit, not withdrawal?
That is exactly what the garden reveals—and exactly what Jesus confirms. The Father still comes walking toward the hiding place. He still asks, *"Where are you?"* not to shame you, but to bring you back into truth, relationship, and life.

Anchor Line

Before man ever learned to overcome the world, he first had to relearn the heart of the God he was hiding from.

And that is where the next section takes us—
because throughout Scripture, the ones who overcame were not the ones who never felt fear...
but the ones who learned to trust the love of God more than the conclusions of the soul.

SECTION 3 — THE OVERCOMING JUDGMENT

How those who walked with God learned to judge by love instead of fear

Core Scripture:
1 John 4:17–18 (KJV) — *"Herein is our love made perfect, that we may have boldness in the day of judgment... There is no fear in love; but perfect love casteth out fear: because fear hath torment. He that feareth is not made perfect in love."*

Eternal judgment is often imagined as a final event—
a courtroom at the end of time,
a verdict after history is over,
a great unveiling that catches humanity off guard.

But Scripture paints something deeper than that.

**Eternal judgment doesn't begin at the end of the earth.
It began before it was formed.**

Before there was dust,
before there was breath in Adam's lungs,
before there was a garden,
there was already a nature in God that did not change.

His judgments were not emotional reactions.
They were not sudden punishments.
They were not divine mood swings.

They were the fixed wisdom of His love.
The dependable boundaries of truth.
The eternal way goodness remains goodness,
freedom remains safe,
and love remains uncorrupted.

That is why those who walked with God did not merely
survive difficult moments.
They learned, often through pressure, pain, delay, injustice,
and uncertainty,
to stop judging by fear
and start judging by the character of God.

They learned to read life through a different lens.

Not through panic.
Not through appearance.
Not through accusation.
Not through the immediate pain of the moment.

But through mercy.
Through compassion.
Through patience.
Through loving-kindness.
Through truth.
Through forgiveness.
Through justice.

In other words—
they learned to judge through the steady light of **Exodus
34:6** long before it was fully revealed in Jesus.

And when Jesus came,
He did not introduce a new way of judgment.
He revealed the eternal one.

1. THE SOUL JUDGES TO SURVIVE — THE SPIRIT LEARNS TO JUDGE TO REMAIN IN LOVE

The soul is fast.

It reads danger quickly.
It scans for rejection.
It predicts pain.
It reacts to uncertainty.
It makes snap conclusions in order to protect itself.

That is not always evil.
Sometimes it is simply human.

But when the soul becomes the highest judge,
fear becomes the measuring rod.

And once fear becomes the judge,
everything begins to bend:

- Delay feels like abandonment.
- Correction feels like rejection.
- Waiting feels like punishment.
- Silence feels like distance.
- Pressure feels like proof that God is not good.

This is why the soul so often misreads the dealings of God.

It does not only fear punishment.
It fears exposure.
It fears loss.
It fears not being enough.
It fears the possibility that it has misunderstood everything.

So it rushes to compensate.
It strives.
It hides.
It performs.

It manages appearances.
It tries to become safe through effort.

But the spirit—
when awakened by the love of God—
begins to learn another way.

The spirit begins to ask:

- What is true here?
- What is God like here?
- What remains dependable here?
- What would love say in this moment?
- What judgment keeps me aligned with His nature
  instead of my panic?

That is the overcoming judgment.

Not the absence of discernment.
Not passivity.
Not pretending pain is not real.

It is the growing ability
to interpret life through the nature of God
instead of through the fear of the soul.

This is why John says:

"Herein is our love made perfect, that we may have boldness in the day of judgment..."

Notice the language.

Not terror.
Not panic.
Not scrambling.
Boldness.

Why?

Because the one who has learned the love of God
has already begun to understand the judgments of God.

And that person is no longer trying to hide from the light.
They are learning to walk in it.

2. ABRAHAM, JOSEPH, DAVID, AND DANIEL — MEN WHO LEARNED TO READ THEIR STORY THROUGH GOD'S NATURE

Throughout Scripture,
the people who overcame were not always the strongest,
the fastest,
or the most naturally gifted.

They were the ones who, over time,
learned to stop letting fear have the final interpretation.

Abraham

Abraham was asked to leave what was familiar
and walk toward what was not yet visible.

That alone is enough to disturb the soul.

No map.
No final blueprint.
No guarantee the journey would be comfortable.
Only the voice of God
and the promise that love had already prepared something
ahead.

Abraham had moments of weakness.
He stumbled.
He tried to help the promise along.

But the deeper pattern remained:

He kept returning to the judgment that **God was trustworthy**.

That is overcoming judgment.

Not perfection in behavior—
but a settled return to the character of God.

Joseph

Joseph was given a dream
and then thrown into a story that looked like the opposite of
the dream.

Betrayed.
Sold.
Falsely accused.
Forgotten.

Every stage gave the soul enough evidence
to conclude that God had failed him.

But Joseph did not let the prison become the final
interpretation.

When the story opened,
he did not judge his brothers through revenge.
He judged the whole journey through providence.

Genesis 50:20 (KJV) — *"But as for you, ye thought evil
against me; but God meant it unto good..."*

That is not naïve optimism.
That is a man whose judgment has been re-formed.

He can distinguish between human evil
and divine goodness
without confusing the two.

He does not call evil good.
But he refuses to let evil become the final word.

That is love judging rightly.

David

David knew what it meant to be anointed
and then hunted.

He knew what it meant to be chosen
and then hidden in caves.

He had multiple opportunities
to solve his pain by stepping outside the judgment of God.

He could have killed Saul.
He could have forced the promise.
He could have made fear his counselor.

But again and again,
David restrained himself at crucial moments
because he refused to seize what God had not released.

That is not weakness.
That is government.

David was learning that true authority
does not prove itself through reaction.

It stays aligned with the timing and nature of God.

Even when David failed deeply later in life,
his path back was not denial.
It was repentance.

And repentance itself
is an act of overcoming judgment—
because it agrees with what is true
without running from the One who is true.

Daniel

Daniel lived under foreign power,
in a system that did not honor his God,
with pressure all around him to compromise.

And yet his judgments remained clear.

He did not become aggressive.
He did not become bitter.
He did not collapse inward.

He simply stayed aligned.

Windows open.
Heart steady.
Spirit fixed.

When lions came,
Daniel was not delivered because he knew a technique.

He was delivered because his life had already been judged
into alignment.

His private decisions
had been training his public courage.

That is how overcoming judgment works.

It is not built in the dramatic moment.
It is built in the quiet agreements before the dramatic
moment arrives.

3. JESUS — THE SUPREME PATTERN OF JUDGMENT WITHOUT FEAR

Every prior example matters.
But all of them are partial until Jesus.

Jesus does not merely teach eternal judgment.
He embodies it.

He is not simply the messenger.
He is the visible revelation
of how the judgments of God actually move when love is
fully mature in a man.

This is why He could say:

John 5:30 (KJV) — *"I can of mine own self do nothing...
as I hear, I judge: and my judgment is just; because I seek
not mine own will, but the will of the Father which hath
sent me."*

This verse is one of the clearest windows in all of Scripture.

Jesus did not judge from ego.
He did not judge from self-protection.
He did not judge from offense.
He did not judge from appearance.
He did not judge from religious pressure.
He did not judge from crowd demand.

He judged from union.

"As I hear, I judge."

That is the language of perfect alignment.

His judgment was not random.
It was relational.

His judgment was just
because it flowed from the Father.

And what was the Father like?

Exodus 34:6 (KJV) —
*"The Lord, The Lord God, merciful and gracious,
longsuffering, and abundant in goodness and truth..."*

That means every judgment of Jesus
was already passing through:

- mercy
- compassion
- patience
- loving-kindness
- truth
- forgiveness
- justice

This is why sinners could come near Him while hypocrites
felt exposed. This is why broken people felt seen
while false systems felt threatened.

This is why He could correct without condemning,
confront without cruelty, and carry authority without fear.

He was not soft because He lacked standards.
He was safe because His standards were perfectly rooted in
love.

That is the overcoming judgment in its full form.

Not weak.
Not vague.
Not permissive.
Not harsh.

Perfectly aligned.

4. "LORD, LORD…" — WHY FINAL JUDGMENT IS NOT GOD SNEAKING UP BEHIND US

One of the most sobering passages in the New Testament is this:

Matthew 7:22–23 (KJV) —
"Many will say to me in that day, Lord, Lord, have we not prophesied in thy name? and in thy name have cast out devils? and in thy name done many wonderful works? And then will I profess unto them, I never knew you: depart from me, ye that work iniquity."

This passage has frightened many people.
And if read through the fear of the soul,
it can sound like God is waiting behind the curtain
to shock people at the end.

But that is not what Jesus is revealing.

God is not sneaking up behind us with a big stick.

He is standing in front of us with a loving rod and a staff.

The issue in Matthew 7 is not that God was absent.
The issue is not that He failed to make Himself known.
The issue is not that His heart was hidden.

The issue is relationship.

"I never knew you."

Not:
"I never saw your works."
Not:
"I never noticed your activity."

Not:
"I forgot your religious effort."

But:
"I never knew you."

This is the difference between activity and alignment.
Between performance and union.
Between power as display
and power as shared life.

Many can do things *around* the name of Jesus
without learning to live *in* His nature.

And this chapter is slowly removing that confusion.

Because eternal judgment is not first about dramatic events
at the end.
It is about the eternal nature of God
becoming the standard by which all things are weighed.

If a man can preach, perform, impress, and influence
without becoming more merciful,
more compassionate,
more patient,
more true,
more forgiving,
more just in love—

then the issue is not gifting.

The issue is union.

And that is why this doctrine matters so deeply.

5. THE OVERCOMING JUDGMENT — LEARNING TO INTERPRET LIFE THROUGH LOVE IN CHRIST

This is where the section becomes deeply personal.

Because most readers are not standing in a lion's den today.
Most are not in Pharaoh's prison.
Most are not hiding in caves from Saul.

But many are facing:

- disappointment
- unanswered questions
- long delays
- painful memories
- spiritual confusion
- condemnation
- internal striving
- fear that they have missed something
- fear that God is disappointed in them
- fear that their pain means they are failing

And this is where the overcoming judgment must become practical.

The question is not:

"Will I ever be judged?"

The deeper question is:

"What lens am I using right now to interpret my life?"

If the lens is fear,
the soul will write dark stories quickly.

If the lens is condemnation,
every correction will feel like rejection.

If the lens is self-protection,
you will resist the very love trying to heal you.

But if the lens becomes **God's love in Christ,**
everything starts to re-order.

Romans says:

Romans 8:1 (KJV) —
*"There is therefore now no condemnation to them which
are in Christ Jesus..."*

And John says:

**"There is no fear in love; but perfect love casteth
out fear..."**

Together, they form a doorway.

No condemnation.
No fear.

Not because nothing matters.
Not because there is no judgment.
But because **the judgment itself is being healed in
Christ.**

This is one of the deepest revelations in the doctrine.

The answer to false judgment
is not the removal of all judgment.

It is the restoration of **right judgment**.

Judgment that sees clearly.
Judgment that stays in truth.
Judgment that agrees with love.

Judgment that can correct without condemning.
Judgment that can discern without hiding.
Judgment that can face the light and remain there.

That is what Jesus is forming in His people.

Not merely people who avoid hell.
But people who learn to see like heaven.

And the more this matures in you,
the less "the day of judgment" feels like a threat
and the more it feels like the unveiling
of what love has been teaching you all along.

GUIDED DISCOVERY — 3 QUESTIONS THAT HELP THE READER RECOGNIZE THE SHIFT

1. When pressure hits your life, what usually interprets the moment first—fear, or the known character of God?

For most people, fear speaks first. That does not make you a failure. It makes you human. But spiritual maturity begins when fear is no longer allowed to be the final interpreter. The overcoming judgment is learning to pause long enough to ask, *What is true here? What is God like here?* Over time, the soul stops reacting alone, and the spirit begins to lead.

2. Have you ever confused God's correction with rejection because your soul still expected condemnation?

Many believers have. That is one of the deepest wounds carried out of Adam's first misaligned judgment. But in

Christ, correction is no longer proof that you are cast away. It is often proof that you are being loved into alignment. The Father disciplines differently than fear predicts. He is not trying to crush you. He is teaching you how to stand.

3. What if the goal of judgment is not to make you afraid of the light—but to make you able to live in it?

This is the shift. Eternal judgment, rightly understood, is not merely a future verdict. It is the eternal wisdom of God training the heart to remain in truth, freedom, and love. The more you learn to judge through God's nature, the less you hide from Him—and the more you become stable in Him. That is why perfect love produces boldness, not panic.

SECTION ANCHOR

The overcoming judgment is the moment the soul stops asking, "How do I protect myself?"
and the spirit begins asking, "What is true in the love of God right now?"

If Section 1 showed why the soul fears judgment,
and Section 2 showed how the first wrong judgment about God taught humanity to hide,
then Section 3 now reveals the pattern of those who overcame:

They learned to interpret life through the nature of God instead of through the panic of the soul.

But one final turn still remains.

Because even this truth can stay abstract
unless the reader sees it fully in Jesus.

Not only as a pattern of discernment...
but as the place where judgment itself becomes liberation.

Because in Christ,
judgment does not only expose what is false.

It separates what is false from you.

And that is where we go next.

SECTION 4 — THE JUDGMENT THAT SETS FREE

When the judgment of God is finally seen through Jesus, it no longer feels like a threat at your back—but a Shepherd calling you forward.

Core Scripture:
John 3:17–21 (KJV) — *"For God sent not his Son into the world to condemn the world; but that the world through him might be saved..."*

There are few doctrines that make the human soul tense faster than the word **judgment**.

Even after years in church, many believers still hear that word and instinctively brace.

They think of punishment.
Exposure.

Rejection.
A verdict waiting somewhere ahead.

But by the time we reach this point in the doctrine, something should already be becoming clear:

God has not been walking us toward fear.
He has been walking us toward **clarity**.

From **repentance from dead works**, we began turning away from the exhausting cycle of self-effort.
Through **faith toward God**, we learned to lean toward His nature instead of our own suspicion.
In **baptisms**, we crossed lines the soul could feel but did not yet fully understand.
In **laying on of hands**, we discovered that God often carries His life through His people.
In **resurrection from the dead**, we saw that His life is not only later—it rises in us now.

And now, at the edge of **eternal judgment**, the question is no longer:

Is God judging?

The deeper question is:

What kind of judgment have we been imagining?

Because if we begin with fear, we will misread the whole thing.
But if we begin with **Jesus**, the whole doctrine starts to come together.

"For God sent not his Son into the world to condemn the world; but that the world through him might be saved."

That one line should settle the room.

Jesus did not come carrying condemnation.
He came carrying **light**.

And light does not arrive first to punish.
It arrives to **reveal**.
To **separate**.
To **align**.
To **liberate**.

The soul hears the word *judgment* and assumes,
Something is about to be held against me.

But the Spirit begins to hear something else:

*God is about to make something clear… so I can finally
walk free.*

1. The Judgment of God Begins With Light, Not Condemnation

Jesus does not introduce judgment by saying, *God came
looking for someone to strike.*

He says **Light came into the world**.

That matters.

Because the first movement of divine judgment is not
random punishment.
It is **illumination**.

Light reveals what darkness hides.
It reveals false conclusions.
Fear-based patterns.
Self-protective striving.
Old agreements the soul made while trying to survive.

And that is why so many people confuse conviction with
rejection.

When light touches a hidden place, the soul often feels exposed and assumes the worst.

But Jesus says the purpose of His coming is not condemnation.

It is salvation.

That means when God reveals what is out of alignment, He is not doing it to shame the willing heart.

He is doing it to rescue it.

This is where the whole doctrine starts to breathe together.

Repentance was never God humiliating you for where you were.
It was His kindness turning you toward life.

Faith toward God was never blind optimism.
It was learning to trust the One who was already reaching for you.

And now **judgment** is not a contradiction of those things.

It is their completion.

Because what God turns you from,
what He teaches you to trust Him in,
what He carries you through,
what He raises alive in you—

He must also **make clear**.

Not to condemn you.
But so you can stop calling darkness home.

2. Romans 8 Draws the Line in the Sand

This is where the doctrine becomes deeply personal.

Romans 8:1–4 (KJV)
"There is therefore now no condemnation to them which are in Christ Jesus... For the law of the Spirit of life in Christ Jesus hath made me free from the law of sin and death..."

This is not just a comforting verse.

This is a **boundary line**.

A crossing.
A transfer.
A line in the sand.

It reaches back into **baptisms** and says:

Something decisive has happened.

A person who is **In Christ** is not simply trying harder under the old government.

He has been brought under a **new law**.

Not the law of sin and death.
But the **law of the Spirit of life in Christ Jesus**.

That is why this passage feels like a spiritual shoreline.

On one side:
condemnation, striving, hiding, fear, Adam, the old reflexes of the soul.

On the other side:
life, liberty, alignment, belonging, Christ, the beginning of a different inner government.

This is not yet the full perfection of the believer.

The soul may still remember Egypt.
But the spirit has been brought into another land.

That line matters.

Because many believers have crossed into Christ spiritually, but still keep interpreting themselves from the wrong side of the water.

They are forgiven, yet still bracing.
Loved, yet still hiding.
Called, yet still compensating.
Alive, yet still listening to death's old accent.

But Romans 8 does not say,
Try to feel less condemned.

It says:

There is therefore now no condemnation to them which are in Christ Jesus.

Not later.
Not eventually.
Not when your performance improves enough to calm your own soul.

Now.

This is the judgment that sets free.

God is not merely declaring what is wrong.

He is declaring which government you now belong to.

And once that line is seen, judgment no longer feels like the closing of a prison door.

It begins to feel like the opening of a gate.

3. Jesus Judges From Union, Not Reaction

If we want to understand how God judges, we do not begin with the fears of Adam.

We begin with **Jesus**.

John 5:22 (KJV)
"For the Father judgeth no man, but hath committed all judgment unto the Son:"

John 5:24 (KJV)
"He that heareth my word, and believeth on him that sent me, hath everlasting life, and shall not come into condemnation; but is passed from death unto life."

John 5:30 (KJV)
"I can of mine own self do nothing... as I hear, I judge: and my judgment is just..."

This is one of the clearest revelations in the whole chapter.

Jesus does not describe judgment as emotional reaction.
He describes it as **perfect union**.

I do not move from Myself.
I do not react from independent will.
I hear.
I align.
I judge from the Father.

That means true judgment is not a knee-jerk response.

It is **aligned perception**.

It is the ability to see what the Father sees and move accordingly.

That is why Jesus could correct without becoming harsh.
Confront without becoming condemning.
Separate darkness from a person without surrendering the person to darkness.

This is not soft compromise.
And it is not religious severity.

This is **truth moving inside love**.

This is what the soul has been searching for all along:

A judgment that is **clean**.
A judgment that is **true**.
A judgment that does not feel like rejection.
A judgment that knows exactly what to remove and exactly what to restore.

And this is where the whole book has been leading in quiet ways.

Repentance teaches us to turn.
Faith teaches us to trust.
Baptism teaches us to cross.
Laying on of hands teaches us to receive.
Resurrection teaches us to live.

But Jesus shows us how all of it becomes **rightly ordered**.

4. The Rod and Staff Are Not Weapons Against the Sheep

Here is where the Shepherd lens heals the doctrine.

Psalm 23:4 (KJV)
"Thy rod and thy staff they comfort me."

That verse only makes sense once judgment has been seen correctly.

Because to the fearful soul, a rod sounds like punishment.

But David says the rod and the staff are a **comfort**.

Why?

Because in the hand of the Shepherd, they are not weapons against the sheep.

They are tools of **protection, rescue, and guidance**.

The rod protects the flock from what would devour it.
The staff reaches for the sheep when it slips, wanders, or becomes entangled.

This is why so much of the fear around judgment begins to dissolve when Jesus becomes the lens.

God is not sneaking up behind you with a big stick.

He is standing before you as a Shepherd.

He is not searching for a reason to crush the willing heart.
He is searching for every way to lead it into safety.

Sometimes that means correction.
Sometimes it means exposure.
Sometimes it means a boundary.
Sometimes it means a redirection.

But none of that is proof of rejection.

Often, it is proof of care.

The Shepherd does not correct because He hates the sheep.
He corrects because cliffs are real.

He does not redirect because He wants control for control's sake.
He redirects because green pastures are real too.

And once the believer begins to understand that, even hard moments start changing shape.

Correction no longer feels like abandonment.
It begins to feel like belonging.

The rod and the staff do not comfort because they are soft.

They comfort because they are **in the right hands**.

5. The Judgment That Sets Free Is the Judgment That Calls You Forward

By the time we arrive here, the doctrine is no longer merely giving us definitions.

It is teaching us how to hear the voice of God correctly.

When Jesus says Light has come, the issue is no longer whether God is willing.

The question is whether the soul will come into what the light reveals.

That is where freedom happens.

Not in pretending.
Not in hiding.
Not in protecting the false self.
Not in defending old agreements.

But in stepping toward what is true.

This is why the judgment of God in Christ is not best understood as a sentence hanging over the believer.

It is better understood as **the loving clarity that refuses to leave him where fear first found him**.

It is the line between Adam and Christ.
Between hiding and coming forth.
Between condemnation and life.
Between the old government and the new.

And as this chapter begins to close, something beautiful should now be settling into the reader:

The God who called us to repent...
the God who taught us to trust...
the God who carried us through the waters...
the God who confirmed and strengthened us through His people...
the God who raised resurrection life within us...

...is not now waiting at the end with a different face.

He is the same Father.
The same Shepherd.
The same Christ.

Which means **eternal judgment** is not the final contradiction of His love.

It is the eternal expression of it.

Guided Discovery — Questions the Soul Wants to Ask but Often Avoids

1. If there is now no condemnation in Christ, why do I still feel condemned sometimes?

Because the spirit may have crossed the line, while the soul is still learning the new land.
Old patterns do not disappear simply because truth has been declared—but they do lose their authority when truth is believed.
Romans 8 is not asking you to manufacture freedom.
It is teaching you where freedom now lives, and under which government you now belong.

2. Is judgment still happening if God is not condemning me?

Yes—but not in the way fear imagines.
In Christ, judgment is no longer the threat of being cast away.
It becomes the loving clarity of God separating what gives life from what keeps you bound.
He is not exposing you to shame you.
He is exposing what is false so you can stop living under it.

3. How do I know if correction is coming from the Shepherd or from accusation?

The enemy exposes to trap, accuse, and drive you inward.
The Shepherd reveals to guide, restore, and call you forward.
One leaves you hiding.
The other leads you into light.
One says, *Stay there and wear this.*
The other says, *Come with Me—this is not your home.*

The judgment of God in Christ is not the condemnation that drives you back—it is the loving clarity that draws you across the line and teaches you how to live free.

And if judgment in Christ is not condemnation...
if Romans 8 has already drawn the line...
if the Shepherd's rod and staff are comforts in the right hands...
if Jesus reveals judgment as alignment with the Father rather than reaction from fear...

...then eternal judgment must be something far deeper than a frightening event at the end.

It must be the **fixed wisdom of God—**
the eternal order that protects freedom, preserves truth, and keeps love safe forever.

And that is where we go now.

SECTION 5 — THE FINAL SEPARATION AND THE INHERITANCE OF LOVE

What cannot remain is finally removed. What is born of God remains forever.

Core Scripture:
**Revelation 21:7 (KJV) — *"He that overcometh shall
inherit all things; and I will be his God, and he
shall be my son."***

There is something in the soul that trembles when it hears
the words *eternal judgment*.
For many, it still sounds like a final courtroom with no
warmth in it—only exposure, rejection, and fear.

But by now, we have walked too far together to stop there.

We have seen that God's judgments are not knee-jerk
reactions.
They are not emotional outbursts.
They are not divine overreactions to human weakness.

They are the fixed wisdom of God.
They are the eternal boundaries of love.
They are the safety rails of truth that protect freedom,
goodness, and life forever.

And if that is true, then the final judgment is not merely the
final condemnation of what is evil.
It is also the final revealing of what is true.
The final removal of what cannot live in God's kingdom.
And the final inheritance of all that was born of His love.

This is where eternal judgment stops sounding like terror to
the one who is In Christ.
And begins sounding like home.

1. Eternal Judgment Does Not Begin
at the End of the Earth

**Before the end was spoken of, the pattern was
already there.**

One of the greatest misunderstandings about eternal judgment is the idea that it only appears at the end of time.

As though God waits until history is over, then suddenly becomes judicial.

But eternal judgment does not begin at the end of the earth. **It began before the earth was formed.**

Before there was man, there was light.
Before there was rebellion, there was order.
Before there was fear, there was the voice of God moving over the deep.

And the first great pattern of judgment in scripture was not destruction.
It was separation.

Genesis 1:3–4 (KJV) — *"And God said, Let there be light: and there was light. And God saw the light, that it was good: and God divided the light from the darkness."*

God brought light into darkness.
He separated what was aligned from what was unaligned.
And He called what was in harmony with His life **good**.

Then He kept going.

He formed.
He ordered.
He divided.
He named.
He blessed.
And when the work was complete, He called it **very good**.

That is not a small detail.
That is the ancient pattern.

Eternal judgment is not merely God deciding what He dislikes.

It is God eternally distinguishing between what can live in
His order and what cannot.

This is why judgment and creation are not enemies in
scripture.
They are companions.

God's judgments are not random acts of condemnation.
They are the ancient wisdom by which He separates what
destroys life from what can live in love.

And we were not only made in that light.
We were made in that image.

We were created to shine.
We were created to carry what is good.
We were created to become, in Him, what heaven always
intended.

That is why eternal judgment is not foreign to the gospel.
It is woven into the very shape of creation itself.

2. The Final Opening of the Books

**What has been hidden will not remain hidden
forever.**

There is a sobering honesty at the center of scripture:
Nothing remains concealed forever.

The soul can hide.
The body can perform.
The mind can justify.
The crowd can applaud what heaven never approved.

But truth has a day.

Revelation 20:12 (KJV) — ***"And I saw the dead, small
and great, stand before God; and the books were***

opened... and the dead were judged out of those things which were written in the books, according to their works."

The books being opened is not God searching for information He did not have.
It is God revealing what was always true.

It is the final unveiling.

Everything hidden behind image, excuse, religion, fear, performance, rebellion, pretense, and self-deception is brought into the light of what it really was.

For the unrenewed soul, that sounds terrifying.
Because the soul survives by managing appearances.

But for the one who has learned to walk In Christ, there is another side to this.
Because what is exposed is not only evil.
What is exposed is also faithfulness.

What was done in secret unto the Father.
What was endured in patience.
What was surrendered in obedience.
What was carried in mercy.
What was offered in compassion.
What was held in truth.
What was forgiven at cost.
What was defended in justice.
What was done from love rather than performance.

Eternal judgment is not only the exposure of darkness.
It is also the public vindication of what was truly born of God.

This is why the final opening of the books is both sobering and holy.

Because at last, all masks come off.
And at last, all reality stands still.

3. The Lamb's Book of Life and the Stories Written In Christ

The deepest security in eternity is not what you achieved, but whose life you are found in.

If the books reveal what was done, the Lamb's Book of Life reveals something even deeper:
belonging.

Revelation 20:15 (KJV) — *"And whosoever was not found written in the book of life was cast into the lake of fire."*

This is where many readers freeze.
And understandably so.

Because the language is severe.
The stakes are final.
And scripture does not soften what is holy.

But this is exactly where the gospel must be heard clearly.

The Lamb's Book of Life is not merely a registry of acceptable people.
It is the testimony that life is found in the Lamb.

This is why scripture keeps drawing us back to the same phrase:

In Christ.

Not merely near Him.
Not merely informed about Him.
Not merely associated with His people.
Not merely speaking His name while resisting His life.

In Christ.

That is the dividing line between religion and union.
That is the difference between familiarity and
transformation.
That is the difference between saying *Lord, Lord* and
actually belonging to the life of the Son.

And the names written in the Lamb's Book of Life are not
just names.
**They are stories, with your name in them—In
Christ.**

They are lives carried by grace.
Lives interrupted by mercy.
Lives reshaped by repentance.
Lives awakened by faith toward God.
Lives brought through the waters.
Lives touched, strengthened, and carried by the hands of
God's people.
Lives learning resurrection before the grave.
Lives finally aligned with eternal judgment because they
learned to love what heaven loves.

This is not cold administration.
This is covenant belonging.

The Lamb's Book of Life is the final testimony that salvation
was never meant to be reduced to a moment, a phrase, or a
religious memory.

It was always meant to become a life.

4. The Overcomer, the Reward, and the Inheritance of Love

Judgment does not only remove what is false. It rewards what remained true.

For many believers, the language of judgment has been preached so heavily through the lens of punishment that they have forgotten something essential:

Judgment in scripture is not only punitive.
It is also vindicating.

It does not only expose rebellion.
It also rewards faithfulness.

It does not only remove what is false.
It honors what remained true.

This is why the end of the story is not merely *depart from me.*
It is also:

Matthew 25:21 (KJV) — *"Well done, thou good and faithful servant... enter thou into the joy of thy lord."*

And again:

Revelation 21:7 (KJV) — *"He that overcometh shall inherit all things; and I will be his God, and he shall be my son."*

This is one of the most important final corrections in the reader's heart.

The overcomer is not the flawless performer.
The overcomer is the one who remains aligned with the life of the Lamb.

The one who keeps turning.
The one who keeps trusting.
The one who keeps crossing.
The one who keeps receiving and giving support.
The one who keeps yielding to resurrection life.
The one who keeps learning the judgments of love until fear
loses its grip.

This is not perfection by the soul.
This is perseverance in union.

And when the final judgment comes, it does not only say,
this cannot remain.
It also says, *this belongs to Me.*

This is where inheritance enters the doctrine.

Not because man earned eternity by performance.
But because what was born of God in him was real.

Mercy matured.
Compassion endured.
Patience held.
Loving-kindness ripened.
Truth remained dependable.
Forgiveness cleared the debt.
Justice defended what was good.

These were not merely virtues discussed in a chapter.
They were the visible grain of a life being shaped by the
nature of the Father.

And what is born of Him can survive His light.

That is why the final judgment is not the end of love.
It is the final settling of all that opposes it, so what was born
of God may remain forever.

5. The City, the Completion of the Doctrine, and the Next Horizon

The end of judgment is not emptiness. It is a people, a city, and the dwelling of God with man.

The final pages of scripture do not end in smoke.
They end in a city.

They do not end with absence.
They end with presence.

They do not end with God far away.
They end with God dwelling with man.

Revelation 21:2–3 (KJV) — *"And I John saw the holy city, new Jerusalem, coming down from God out of heaven, prepared as a bride adorned for her husband.
And I heard a great voice out of heaven saying, Behold, the tabernacle of God is with men, and he will dwell with them..."*

This matters more than many realize.

Because the final image of eternity is not isolated souls floating in private spirituality.
It is a prepared people.
A holy city.
A bride.
A dwelling.
A structure.
A habitation.

In other words:
the final image of eternity is not merely *saved individuals*.

It is **the fulfilled design of God in community**.

And suddenly the six doctrines of Hebrews 6 do not feel like disconnected teachings at all.

They feel like a path.

Repentance from dead works taught us to turn from what cannot give life.
Faith toward God taught us where to face and where true life is found.
The doctrine of baptisms taught us that crossing is real, and what is old cannot remain untouched.
Laying on of hands taught us that God does not form isolated believers, but a people who carry, bless, confirm, and build one another.
Resurrection from the dead taught us that His life is not only later, but rising in us now.
Eternal judgment has now shown us the final settling of all things—the removal of what cannot remain, the reward of what was born of God, and the inheritance of those who remain In Christ.

This was never six disconnected doctrines.
This was one journey into maturity.

And maturity is not merely information.
It is alignment.

It is a life that increasingly agrees with heaven.
A life that learns to love what God loves.
A life that becomes safe for His presence, useful in His purpose, and ready for His kingdom.

That is why this chapter must not end in dread.
It must end in design.

Because the final judgment is not God turning off the light.
It is God removing forever what cannot live in it.
And for those who remain In Christ, it is not merely survival.

It is inheritance.
It is home.

Living the Very Good Life showed us the blueprint for the
body, soul, and spirit.
The Doctrine of Christ has shown us God's blueprint from
repentance to eternal alignment.
The Body of Christ reveals the greater blueprint still—God's
blueprint for eternal life.

The Doctrine of Christ has shown us the path into maturity.
But maturity is not the end of the journey—it is the horizon
where the next one begins.
The next horizon is not merely what happens to the believer.
It is what happens when the believer becomes part of the
living structure God has always intended—
The Body of Christ.

Guided Discovery

**1. Why does scripture end with a city instead of just
individuals?**
Because God's final intention has always been larger than
private salvation.
He is building a people, a dwelling, a bride, and a living
structure fit for His presence.

**2. Why do the six doctrines matter so much in light
of the city?**
Because they are not merely introductory teachings to
memorize.
They are foundational alignments that prepare the believer
to become part of what God is building.

**3. What is the true emotional ending of eternal
judgment for the believer?**
Not dread.
Not uncertainty.
Not endless religious anxiety.

For the one who remains In Christ, the true ending is
belonging, inheritance, and home.

The end of judgment is not emptiness.
It is the city of God filled with those who learned to live in
His love.

CHAPTER 6 CLOSE — ETERNAL JUDGMENT

The final settling of love, and the doorway into what comes next

If eternal judgment has been feared, it is often because it has been taught without the face of the Father.

Separated from His nature, judgment sounds like threat.
Separated from Christ, it sounds like rejection.
Separated from love, it sounds like a future humanity can only dread.

But now the doctrine stands clearer.

Eternal judgment is not the final collapse of hope. It is the final settling of truth.

It is the full unveiling of what was always true.
The final removal of what cannot live in God's kingdom.
The public exposure of what was hidden.
The vindication of what was faithful.
The rewarding of what was born of God.
And the inheritance of those who remain In Christ.

This is why the doctrine must never be preached as terror alone.

Yes, it is sober.
Yes, it is final.
Yes, it reveals that what resists God's life cannot remain forever.

But it is also holy.
It is also just.
It is also good.
And for the believer learning to walk in union with Christ, it is deeply reassuring.

Because the same God who divided light from darkness in the beginning has never changed.
The same God who called what was aligned with Him *good* still has not changed.
The same God who kept going until creation became *very good* is still working toward His end.

His judgments are not emotional reactions.
They are eternal wisdom.

They are the safety rails of freedom.
The boundaries of life.
The structure of love.
The settled ways of the kingdom that make communion, trust, goodness, and joy possible forever.

And if that is true, then eternal judgment is not the strange final doctrine at the end of Hebrews 6.

It is the final confirmation that every other doctrine mattered.

Repentance mattered because direction matters.
Faith mattered because union matters.
Baptisms mattered because crossing matters.
Laying on of hands mattered because God builds through people.
Resurrection mattered because His life must rise in us now and triumph fully at the end.
And eternal judgment matters because what is true must finally stand, what is false must finally fall, and what is born of God must finally remain.

This is why the end of the doctrine is not merely warning.
It is clarity.

Not merely consequence.
But completion.

Not merely the closing of a book.
But the settling of a foundation.

And the names written in the Lamb's Book of Life are not just names.
They are stories, with your name in them—In Christ.

That is the hope.
That is the sobriety.
That is the comfort.
That is the invitation.

Not merely to survive the end.
But to become, even now, the kind of life that agrees with heaven.

And that is why this book must end where it does.

Because *The Doctrine of Christ* is not the final destination.
It is the maturing path.

It teaches us how to turn.
How to trust.
How to cross.

How to receive and carry support.
How to live resurrection now.

And how to understand the final settling of all things
through the lens of God's love rather than religious fear.

But maturity is not the end of the journey.

It is the horizon where the next one begins.

The next horizon is not merely what happens to the believer.
It is what happens when the believer becomes part of the
living structure God has always intended.

A people.
A dwelling.
A bride.
A city.
A body.

The Body of Christ.

And so we do not leave this doctrine looking backward in
dread.
We leave it looking forward in alignment.

Not only asking,

How do I avoid judgment?
But learning to ask, *How do I become the kind of person
who can live in the city?*

Not asking only, *How do I get through the fire?*
But learning to ask, *What in me is already being shaped for
the light?*

Not asking only, *What happens at the end?*
But learning to ask, *What is God building now?*

That is the true handoff.

Living the Very Good Life showed us the blueprint for the
body, soul, and spirit.
The Doctrine of Christ has shown us God's blueprint from
repentance to eternal alignment.
The Body of Christ reveals the greater blueprint still—God's
blueprint for eternal life.

So the foundation is laid.
The lines are marked.
The frame is rising.

And now the horizon opens.

Continue the journey:

1. Discover God's Love — *The Book of Christ*

2. Learn to Live In Christ — *The Doctrine of Chris*

3. Grow in the Body — *The Body of Chris*

4. Walk in the Gifts — *The Gifts of Christ*

For more resources, teachings, and related works, visit <u>bodyofchrist.online</u>